ON THE MOOR

ON THE MOOR

Science, History and Nature on a Country Walk

Richard Carter

Published by Gruts Media.

richardcarter.com/on-the-moor/

ISBN-13:   978-1979518840
ISBN-10:   197951884X

For Jen, who introduced me to the Moor; and in memory of my mum, Brenda Carter, who introduced me to wheatears.

Contents

Prologue

Way down in the southern hemisphere, the ocean floor slips beneath Laurentia. Farther yet to the south, near the edge of the Antarctic Circle, the shrinking seabed tugs loose a splinter from Gondwana, the southern supercontinent. The splinter, Avalonia, heads north on a collision course with Laurentia. She travels at a breakneck five centimetres per year: twice as fast as fingernails will some day grow.

When it comes to collisions, it is not speed that counts, but momentum. We are heading for one hell of a crash. Avalonia comprises sections of the earth's crust which will one day become England, Wales, southern Ireland, Belgium, the Netherlands, and small sections of France, Germany, Poland and the eastern seaboard of North America. But Avalonia is minuscule compared to Laurentia: the combined future landmasses of most of the United States, Canada, Greenland, northern Ireland, and Scotland.

After an 80-million-year, 4,500-kilometre journey north, Avalonia hurtles into Laurentia. In the process,

England ploughs into Scotland: the mother of all Acts of Union. Mountains rise in the Caledonian and Cumbrian crumple-zones, some of them rivalling the Himalaya—although the Himalaya will not exist for another third of a billion years.

Shallow seas form, laying down coral: the limestone of the Yorkshire Dales and Derbyshire. The towering young mountains erode. County-loads of sediment are deposited in equatorial river deltas: God's own millstone grit; Yorkshire made from Scotland. Tree-ferns and giant lycopods thrive and die in shifting swamps: the coal measures. Amphibians and early reptiles hop, crawl and speciate in humid forests. Giant insects rule the air. Trilobites infest the seas. Plants rampage across the world, scrubbing carbon from the atmosphere. Carbonates precipitate. The planet cools. Ice comes to Gondwana.

Locked together, for the time being at least, Laurentia and Avalonia drift into the northern hemisphere. They near the Tropic of Cancer, and swamp turns to desert: the red sandstone of Cheshire and Lancashire. But the conjoined landmasses do not travel alone: colossal Gondwana follows close on their heels.

Ker-thud! Gondwana rams into Laurentia. The Appalachians, Pyrenees and Urals rise as the world's continents coalesce. A single ocean laps the shores of united Pangea. Avalonia lies landlocked in the arid heart of the world.

Without warning, something terrible happens—the

most terrible event ever to befall life on Earth: 96% of marine species, 70% of landlubbers, gone in the geological blink of an eye. But life is good at finding new ways. The trilobites are lost forever, but the disaster clears niches for enterprising young species to exploit. The Age of the Dinosaurs is upon us.

Now a vast bay of Panthalassa, the All-Sea, encroaches into the land. Shallow seas form, filled with ichthyosaurs, plesiosaurs and ammonites. Pangea begins to split. A great Atlantic rent unzips, tearing through the heart of Avalonia: a proto-Britain on one side, the long-lost land of Newfoundland on the other.

The newborn ocean ridges and spreads. The earth shakes. Chalk precipitates from the seas.

Now, another disaster, not as great as the last, but devastating nevertheless: no more giant sea-reptiles; no more ammonites; no more dinosaurs, except for a few with feathers. Niches are cleared once more. Stand aside! Here we come, we lucky mammals!

Africa shunts into Europe, India into Asia: the Alps and Himalaya are born. The planet cools. Africa dries. Apes stand upright and learn to run. Ice comes and goes, seas fall and rise, over and over. Man arrives on the British peninsula, bringing fire and axe. The ice melts, and the seas rise once more. We are an island. More men come, and see, and conquer.

The rest, as they say, is history.

Introduction

Walking with Minerva

If the Pennines really are *the backbone of England*, then the Moor, high above Hebden Bridge in West Yorkshire, is somewhere on the twelfth thoracic vertebra. That's the one next to the adrenal glands at the top of the kidneys. The vertebra to which the final pair of ribs is attached. *False ribs*, as they're called. The most convenient rib, surely, for God to have removed from Adam's side to fashion into Eve. If He ever did. Which He didn't.

Some of the pedlars of alternative therapies down in the valley would have you believe that the twelfth thoracic vertebra is the location of the *solar plexus chakra*: a centre of vitality associated with strong desires and emotions, a healthy digestive system, and the colour yellow. Others will tell you it's an acupressure point for treating diabetes. Yet others will claim a *misalignment* of the twelfth thoracic vertebra is associated with rheumatism, indigestion pains, and sterility. The homeopaths won't fill your head with any such nonsense, although they might try to flog you a few sugar-pills.

Which is why I stick to the Moor. It's the only alternative therapy I need. A couple of hours up there, and all is right with the world. Feeling a bit listless? Irked by something trivial? Not sure how to start the introduction to your book? Stop wittering, get up on to the Moor, and sort yourself out!

The Moor is a great place for thinking; for observing the changing seasons; for getting a bit of fresh air. It is high, and wide, and surprisingly flat, and—best of all—pretty much empty most of the time. Empty save for heather and grouse, and the occasional nutter in running shoes.

Pliny the Younger had it right. We worked our way through some of his early-first-millennium correspondence in Spiny Norman's late-second-millennium Latin classes. The first of Pliny's letters in our textbook was to his friend the historian Tacitus. *Ridebis et licet rideas*, he begins: "You will laugh, and laugh you may: I, the man you know so well, have captured three boars—and three very fine boars at that!" Pliny goes on to describe a boar-hunting epiphany: how sitting, waiting at the boar-nets had afforded him an opportunity to reflect, and make notes. "There is something, too," he writes, "in the solemnity of the venerable woods surrounding you, together with that profound silence which is observed on these occasions, which forcibly disposes the mind to meditation." Pliny sums up this surprising revelation with a poetic flourish, observing that the goddess of wisdom, Minerva, is just as likely to be found roaming the hills as is the goddess of hunting, Diana.

There are no venerable woods on the Moor these days. If there were, it wouldn't be a moor. There are no wild boar either. They were hunted to extinction long ago. But there are still ample opportunities to enjoy the Moor's solemnity and silence, and even to meditate. Or, better still, just to let your feet and mind wander where they will: *rambling* in both senses of the word; *ruminating*, like the sheep.

We have more moors than you can shake a stick at around here. They're everywhere you look: Soyland Moor and Stansfield Moor, Widdop Moor and Warley Moor, Oxenhope Moor and Ovenden Moor. And those are just some of the moors you can actually see from here—see to shake a stick at. There are plenty of other moors farther out, moors beyond moors: Stanbury Moor, where Heathcliff schemed and brooded; Ilkley Moor, where folk go without hats, and where Charles Darwin twisted his ankle; and an entire national park north of York, frequently misdubbed *The Yorkshire Moors*, as if there were no others.

To the people who live near a moor, the local moor is always *the* moor. But, unless they live near *our* moor, they are mistaken. Our moor is *the* Moor: *Moor* with a capital M.

All right, if you want to be pedantic, the Moor is actually two moors: Midgley Moor to the east, and

Wadsworth Moor to the west. But the Moor is not parochial: there's no barbed wire to demarcate the parish boundary, no border control, and no dotted line in the heather. When you're at altitude, observing the natural lie of the land, it's clearly one moor, not two. Hence the singular.

Those crazy Americans, and certain folk down south who have never seen a hill, seem to think that a moor is some sort of drained marsh or fen. Let's nip that nonsense in the bud straight away. A moor is a large tract of open, uncultivated upland, usually acidic, usually covered in heather. The word is Germanic in origin, from the Old English *mór*, meaning *moor*. So let that be an end to it. They can quote *Beowulf* as much as they like, they're wrong: a moor is not a dried-out marsh.

The bedrock of the West Yorkshire moors is of millstone grit: a dark, carboniferous sandstone formed from deep river deltas 300 million years ago. The rock's dark grey, sometimes almost black colour is due to natural weathering. We have an awful lot of weather up here. The colour is not, as many people seem to think, soot from our former *dark, satanic mills*. If you can bring yourself to break a chunk of millstone grit apart, you'll find it to be a silvery or light-biscuity colour inside. A rough, rather grim exterior with a heart of gold—much like the good folk who live in these parts.

Covering most of the millstone grit is a poor, acidic, often boggy soil, mostly peat, in which grows heather, cotton grass, bilberry, moss, rushes, and not much else— unless you look very closely. Which is why, from a financial point of view, the moors are suitable only for grazing a few free-range sheep and cattle, and for grouse-shooting. The least said about incentives for covering our clouded hills in wind turbines the better.

Our local moors are separated by steep, narrow valleys. It's quite a climb to get on to them, but, once you're up there, the tops are, as I said, surprisingly flat. The former river delta has been raised to form what is, in effect, a plateau (technically it's a flat-topped *anticline*), around 300 metres above sea-level. So, when you're out walking, all the hard work comes early on. Once you've gained the height and reached the tops, the going is pretty easy, albeit often wet.

My own favourite walk—I call it *the Moor Walk* (capital M, capital W)—takes me from the house, up to the top of the lane, across the golf course, and up on to the Moor. Then, it's past the old quarries, through the stile, along the paved track through the bog, and a short scramble up to the trig point. Having taken in the view, I then head north along the narrow path through the heather, veer left at the first grouse-shooting butt, then head down past the shooters' hut and through the gate off the Moor. My way home takes me down rough, winding farm tracks, across the road at the pub, and on until the road becomes track once more. At the end of the track, it's a couple of hundred metres back up the road to the house. In all, the walk is about 3.4 miles. If I walked briskly, I could probably do it in an hour and a half. But who wants to walk briskly? *Briskly* is not what the Moor Walk is about.

There are variations on the walk. And there's *the Old Moor Walk*, which starts from the other end of the Moor, and which also has its variations. It's the walk I used to go on before Jen and I bought our home together—the walk from her old house. I sometimes drive over that way to do the Old Moor Walk for old times' sake. Or, if I'm feeling particularly energetic, I'll occasionally merge the two Moor Walks into one.

Very occasionally.

This book is about some of my excursions on the Moor, the things I saw, and the ramblings and ruminations they inspired.

I hope you enjoy it.

Richard Carter
richardcarter.com

Niche

Most of the best walks are circular. Most of the best walks get the climbing over with as soon as possible. The Moor Walk satisfies both these criteria. The first half mile is the killer: out of the house and up the steep lane. It's hard to believe they send buses up here. But I'm an old hand at this game: the secret is to find your own pace and just keep going, stopping only to pretend to admire the view while sneaking a sly breather.

On the route I tend to follow, the Moor could be said to start in one of three places. The first heather appears just beyond the former *Mount Skip Inn*. That was the pub where Ray Winstone crashed his Jag and had a fist-fight in the film *Fanny and Elvis*. What do you mean you've never heard of it? It's a *rom-com* classic! A former packhorse-trail inn, the place is a B&B now: one of innumerable country pubs that have gone to the wall, thanks to drink-driving laws, cheap supermarket booze, and smoking bans. It would have been our local, but we didn't live over here back then. Not a bad pub, from what I remember of the handful of times I drank there.

The land behind Mount Skip is certainly moorland. Indeed, it must once have been part of the Moor, and is still attached to it in a roundabout sort of way. But it was almost entirely cut off from the main body of the Moor when they built the golf course. So I tend to think of it as a forgotten outpost of the Moor, rather than part of the Moor itself. Besides, it goes by a different name: the rather apt *Little Moor*.

Across the cattle grid and the golf course car park, and I arrive at the gate and stile, with its view through the gap towards Pendle Hill. They're an odd lot out that way. They hang witches, apparently. That's Lancashire for you. I'm undeniably on proper moorland beyond this point, as I take a sharp right and join the *Calderdale Way*, passing disused, heather-reclaimed quarries on my left, and an evil-looking par three on my right. Yes, this certainly counts as moorland all right: heather, millstone grit, mud track, and meadow pipits flitting about pretending to be twites.

But then there's the second gate and stile a couple of hundred metres along the track. Beyond here, I'll be on open moorland. This, for me, is the start of *the Moor proper*. I always pause at the gate to take in the view (and to catch another sly breather). It's been a steep, steady climb all the way from the house, but my route is about to level off for a while, before one final brief ascent.

I lean on the gate. To my right, to the south, the valley drops away invisibly beyond the fence. Across the valley lies Cragg Vale, one-time haunt of a gang of murderous coiners. They caught and hanged the ringleader in the end. He's buried across the way in Heptonstall churchyard. A bit of a local folk-hero, by all accounts. That's Yorkshire for you.

Returning my gaze to the route ahead, I look across the boggy flat towards the final slope. This is my first real opportunity to assess how muddy I'm likely to get today. The sheep are the give-away: if they're looking hunched and miserable, the chances are I'll soon be stepping gingerly from tuft to tuft through a few dozen metres of temporary wetland towards the slightly-too-short, stone-flagged path through the bog.

Having satisfied myself the sheep aren't looking particularly miserable today, I turn to inspect the Niche. *The Niche* is my name for a large fence-post, about five feet high and twelve inches across. I make no apologies for employing obsolete imperial units: the post must surely have been measured in feet and inches by whoever set it here years ago. The fence is supported by many such posts spaced at regular intervals along its length, with smaller posts providing additional support in between. The Niche is an end-post, at the break in the fence to accommodate the gate and stile. As such, it has to take more strain than other posts, being pulled from one side, rather than having counterbalancing forces pulling on it in opposite directions.

But it's not this extra workload that makes the Niche special to me, nor that warrants my giving it a name. The Niche is noteworthy because of its hollow top. The centre of the post has rotted away over the years, creating a cylindrical bowl with a two-inch rim. This bowl has become an overgrown plant pot, brimming with grasses, rushes, bilberry, and moss, all struggling for survival in its fifty square inches of real estate. The rotted wood has created an environmental niche for species to exploit; a mini-amphitheatre in which they fight for precious limited resources; a miniature elevated garden to gladden the eye of the passer by. Well, this passer by at least.

It never ceases to amaze me how life finds new places to make a living. Plants, it must be said, don't have much choice in the matter. They can only grow where their seeds happen to land. But they are resourceful, and make the best of the hand dealt to them. A hollowed-out fence post might not be an ideal place to grow, but it provides shelter, nutrients, water, sunlight, and air.

What more does a plant need? If a seed happens to come to rest there, and the conditions are right, a plant will grow. That's what plants do. That's what plants have been doing for hundreds of millions of years.

The dispersal mechanisms of plants—how they find new places to live—was a subject of considerable interest to Charles Darwin. He knew that, for his theory of evolution by means of Natural Selection to be accepted, he needed to explain how species might spread across the planet. If, as according to his theory, closely related species evolved from a common ancestor, how could they so often have ended up in very different, widely dispersed locations? Obviously, this isn't such a great problem for animals, which can at least move—although animal dispersal also gave Darwin one or two headaches—but he also needed to explain how plants might spread to new locations. In particular, how do plants cross oceans? The sea is an extremely inhospitable environment for many plants.

In search of answers to this conundrum, Darwin spent a few years prior to the publication of *On the Origin of Species* investigating mechanisms for plant dispersal. Some of his investigations smacked of obsession. A few seemed to border on down-right crazy. But, as usual, Darwin knew what he was doing.

Received wisdom had it that most plant seeds wouldn't germinate after being exposed to salt water. Darwin decided to put received wisdom to the test. He filled dozens of small bottles with brine and placed different types of seeds in each, letting them soak for varying amounts of time before planting them in dishes in his study. To his delight, nearly all of the seeds grew into healthy plants, even after several days' immersion. But, being Darwin, he didn't stop there. He wrote to one of his naturalist contacts, asking him to try leaving seeds in real sea water, just in case his home-made salt water wasn't a valid substitute. He wrote to the former British consul in the Azores, requesting specimens of the exotic seeds that were known to wash up on the local beaches. Darwin's closest friend and confidant, the ever-sceptical botanist Joseph Dalton Hooker, identified the seeds as Caribbean in origin, planted them, and, to his "unutterable mortification", watched them germinate. Not wishing to miss a trick, Darwin even took the trouble to write to his cousin, asking him to perform similar experiments on lizards' eggs.

Almost as an afterthought, Darwin suddenly realised there was a fundamental problem with his hypothesis that seeds could be transported between continents by bobbing along in ocean currents: most of the seeds in his experiments sank! So, becoming more obsessive, he embarked on a second series of experiments to test other ways in which seeds might be transported over great distances. He floated fruit-laden branches in a tank of salt water; they rotted and sank. He tried feeding oats to fish, reasoning that the seeds might thus pass safely through a conveniently itinerant heron; the fish spat them out. He inspected the feet of freshly shot grouse and ducks for seed-bearing mud; he did indeed find seeds, and managed to germinate them. He retrieved more seeds from bird droppings and pellets; these germinated too. He even floated a dead pigeon with a crop full of seeds in salt water for a month; once again, the seeds germinated. The house stank of artificial sea water. Darwin's poor, adoring wife, Emma, must have had the patience of a saint.

The seeds that grew into the plants living on my favourite fence-post didn't have far to travel: such plants grow in abundance on the Moor. One thing I have noticed, however, is that, whenever I see a fence-post garden like the Niche, it almost invariably contains a small bilberry bush. While many of the plants growing on top of these posts will have grown from wind-blown seeds, the bilberries' seeds were carried there. The small fruits of the bilberry, so fiddly and difficult for us humans to reach, are eaten in their thousands by birds such as red grouse and wheatears. When they're not stuffing their faces with bilberries, these birds tend to use fence-posts as convenient perches, there being few other elevated vantage points on the Moor. When the birds take a dump, the bilberry seeds are deposited in the post-top hollows inside a dollop of fresh fertiliser. Not a bad start in life, if you happen to be a plant. Although perhaps not good enough. It depends on which other plants manage to establish themselves in your fence-post. Make no bones about it, there's a war going on in there: every square inch of the Niche is a battleground, in which individual plants strive to control and exploit the available resources.

In *On the Origin of Species*, Darwin uses a famous simile to illustrate his concept of a *struggle for existence*:

Nature may be compared to a yielding surface, with ten thousand sharp wedges packed close together and driven inwards by incessant blows, sometimes one wedge being struck, and then another with greater force.

For some reason, Darwin groupie that I unashamedly am, I've never been enamoured of his wedge simile. Maybe Darwin wasn't either: he removed it from subsequent editions of his book. But it crosses my mind every time I look down into the Niche's botanic garden: all those organisms packed into the tiniest of spaces, competing for light and nutrients.

It so happens, Darwin came up with his wedge simile during one of the great *eureka moments* in the history of science—although I should, perhaps, point out that modern historians of science tend to pooh-pooh the very idea of eureka moments. This particular eureka moment occurred on 28th September 1838, when, as Darwin explained in his autobiography over four decades later (getting the month wrong, and, it has been suggested, misremembering the sudden nature of the revelation):

In October 1838, that is, fifteen months after I had begun my systematic enquiry, I happened to read for amusement 'Malthus on Population,' and being well prepared to appreciate the struggle for existence which everywhere goes on from long-continued observation of the habits of animals and plants, it at once struck me that under these circumstances favourable variations would tend to be preserved, and unfavourable ones to be destroyed.

Darwin's idea of what constituted an amusing read might seem odd to modern readers, but fortune favours the prepared mind. Thanks to observations he had made during and after his five-year voyage around the world aboard *HMS Beagle*, Darwin was already convinced, as others had been before him, that species evolve. But he, like the rest of them, lacked a physical mechanism by which evolution might occur. Reading the Reverend Thomas Malthus's essay on the dangers of human population growth, Darwin realised he now had such a mechanism: a *struggle for existence*, in which better-adapted individuals stand a better chance of surviving and reproducing. He dubbed this mechanism *Natural Selection* (in contrast to *artificial selection*: the selective breeding employed by humans to develop desirable traits in domesticated plants and animals). In the same notebook in which Darwin recorded Malthus's key points, he also jotted down some initial thoughts of his own, and the wedge simile was born:

One may say there is a force like a hundred thousand wedges trying [to] force every kind of adapted structure into the gaps in the economy of nature, or rather forming gaps by thrusting out weaker ones.

Such struggles for existence are going on all the time in the natural world, be they in the Galápagos Islands, the

Serengeti, or on top of a fence-post on the edge of a Yorkshire moor. That's the real power and beauty of Darwin's great theory of evolution by means of Natural Selection: its universality. It's happening right now, everywhere there's life, even though it might not always look that way. When I look down into the Niche, I don't see a struggle for existence, but that, most assuredly, is what I'm looking at.

Post mortem

On my next walk up to the Moor after writing this chapter, I discovered that the fence marking the start of *the Moor proper* had been replaced. The fence-post I had nicknamed *the Niche* had been pulled up; a pristine, sterile new one stood in its place—a post, no doubt, measured in metric units.

Things wear out. Things rot away. In the great war against entropy, things need to be replaced. The people who put up the new fence made a good job of it, but their fix can only be temporary. How long before their new fence-posts begin to absorb water and start to rot? How long before a bilberry-laden wheatear lands on one of those posts and drops a load? How long before small bushes begin to sprout from new post-top gardens? Not long is my guess.

That's what bilberry bushes do.

Urnfield

Over the stile and on to the Moor proper.

For a change, I turn right and follow the fence down the slope. I've decided to look for the mysterious *Enclosure* marked in Gothic typeface on the Ordnance Survey map: the typeface denoting archaeological monuments.

There's no path as such, but I don't have far to walk through the fading, late-September heather. And there it is, just short of where the fences meet at the corner of the Moor: a large, low, circular bank, topped with heather, its inner circumference highlighted by yellowing moor-grass—that is, by an absence of heather.

The enclosure is impressive, much bigger than I imagined, but I can't help feeling that, had I not been looking for it, I might have walked straight past without giving it a second glance: a discreet patch of regularity subsumed into the tussocky irregularity of the Moor.

I step up on to the bank for a better view. The perimeter is easier to make out from up here, curving away to left and right, meeting again on the far side.

There appears to be a raised, heather-capped hub in the centre of the circle. I walk towards it, counting my paces, continuing across to the opposite point on the circumference, the *antipodal* point: 36 paces of my 29-inch legs; 30 metres, give or take.

The bank seems more elevated here: I had to step up higher to climb on to it. Then I realise the inner edge of the bank has a shallow, barely discernible depression running along its base: I had to step up higher because I was standing in the remains of a ditch.

Until I began researching it a few days ago, I'd assumed that the map's Gothic *Enclosure* recorded the location of a medieval pen for holding livestock. Sheep, most likely. What else would you need to enclose around here? Then I learnt that the first edition of the Ordnance Survey map for the area, published in 1851, marks the site as a "British Camp (Supposed)". I was, of course, immediately intrigued. Further research on Calderdale Council's online *Register of Ancient Monuments* revealed that the circular earthwork is, in fact, a late Bronze Age burial ground: an *urnfield* in which, around 3,000 years ago, ancient Britons interred the cremated remains of their dead in funerary pots. As soon as I read this, I knew I had to come up here to pay my respects.

I return to the centre of the circle and step up on to the hub. It certainly feels like a deliberate feature, rather than some random hummock. I turn slowly through 360 degrees, then 720. What on earth would possess someone to build a burial ground all the way up here, in the middle of nowhere? And such a large burial ground at that. You could get an awful lot of urns into a 30-metre-diameter circle.

But why *not* have a burial ground up here? The urnfield, it now occurs to me, has a commanding view over the valley, despite its relatively low position on the Moor. It's built on a natural terrace which juts out from the main bulk of the Moor, affording a 180° panoramic view to the south. There could be far worse places to spend eternity. Perhaps our Bronze Age predecessors appreciated an imposing view as much as the rest of us, and wanted the best for their departed loved ones.

Yes, *loved ones*... These were real people, we forget that. The people who made this urnfield ate and drank, laughed and cried, loved and argued, toiled and ached, made plans and had children, grew ill and died. They sweated in the sun, they shivered in the rain, they blew on their fingers when it snowed. They were *alive*. They lived right here, in their now. Their lives were every bit as important and eventful to them as ours are to us. Yet we know almost nothing about them. Archaeology might tell us when they lived, and what they ate, and about some of the things they made, but it can never tell us their names, or what they believed, or what songs they sang. That information, once so precious to these real, living and breathing people, has been turned to corruption; lost forever, as all our precious information will one day be lost. Entropy always wins. There is no backup, no way to retrieve what has been lost. All that's left is conjecture and supposition.

Few things irritate me more... No, that's putting it

too strongly. One of life's minor irritations, which irks me far more than it should, is when people with an interest in a particular subject start to invent crazy hypotheses based on little or no evidence. The irritation is magnified when their hypotheses encroach into areas I also happen to be interested in: science, say, or history, or archaeology. *Heisenberg's Uncertainty Principle* does not, in any way, validate homeopathic 'theory'; Charles Darwin had nothing to say on the subject of business practice, finance, or literary criticism (other than finding Shakespeare so "intolerably dull" that it nauseated him); recent discoveries concerning ancient tsunamis do not mean that Moses really parted the Red Sea. It's all bollocks. Don't listen to them. In this postmodern age, anyone, it seems, is entitled to come up with crackpot hypotheses. Which is what I find myself doing right now:

As I complete my second panoramic scan from the middle of the urnfield, I notice, as I've often noticed before, just how flat the horizon is from up here. Yes, there are undulations and discontinuities in the millstone grit plateau, but, even from this relatively low position, it all seems remarkably level—especially if you keep your eyes on the horizon and don't look down into the valley. I am, it occurs to me, standing at the centre of an ancient, circular monument with a wide view across what is, in effect, a flat landscape. In this respect, it's much like the view from Stonehenge—albeit without the monoliths. And the view is southwards, towards the sun. Is it possible this urnfield could have served two purposes: the first as a burial ground; the second, like

Stonehenge and other ancient monuments, as some sort of calendar? This would be an ideal location for observing the changing positions of sunrise and sunset throughout the year, aligning them with features on the horizon. *When the sun rises behind that crag, it's time for the autumn feast; when it sets through that notch, the nights will start to grow longer once more.* I can easily imagine the urnfield serving such a double purpose.

But it's just that: *imagination.*

HYDRIOTAPHIA, URNE-BURIALL, OR, A Difcourfe of the Sepulchrall Urnes lately found in NORFOLK is how Thomas Browne, *D. of Phyfick*, entitles his great 1658 essay. He uses the recent discovery and excavation of an urnfield in Old Walsingham, thirty miles from his home in Norwich, as an opportunity to discuss the burial practices of societies both ancient and modern. He closes with a moving and erudite final chapter, expounding on the vanity and ultimate futility of attempting to leave lasting memorials:

> *Who hath the oracle of his ashes, or whither they are to be scattered? The relicks of many lie like the ruins of Pompey's, in all parts of the earth.*

No matter how hard we might try to secure a lasting record of our names and deeds, once we're gone, argues Browne, the survival of such memorials is subject to blind chance, and the whims and vagaries of time:

Herostratus lives that burnt the temple of Diana, he is almost lost that built it. Time hath spared the epitaph of Adrian's horse, confounded that of himself... Who knows whether the best of men be known, or whether there be not more remarkable persons forgot, than any that stand remembered in the known account of time? The first man had been as unknown as the last, and Methuselah's long life had been his only chronicle... [T]he iniquity of oblivion blindly scattereth her poppy, and deals with the memory of men without distinction to merit of perpetuity.

Yet Browne's urns, *these sad and sepulchral pitchers*, buried *not a yard deep* have somehow survived, where great mausoleums have not: "Time, which antiquates antiquities, and hath an art to make dust of all things, hath yet spared these minor monuments"—albeit we don't know whose monuments they are.

Thomas Browne was a genuine polymath. Born in London on 19th October (or possibly 19th November) 1605, he obtained two degrees from Oxford, then travelled to the continent to study different approaches to medicine at the major medical centres of Montpellier, Padua and Leyden. While waiting for his Leyden doctorate to be incorporated by Oxford University, he spent the years 1634–37 practicing medicine from Shibden Hall near Halifax—just six miles east of where I stand, like Browne, contemplating an ancient urnfield. It was at Shibden Hall that Browne wrote the original version of the book that first brought him to notice and acclaim: *Religio Medici* (*The Religion of a Doctor*). He didn't initially intend the work for publication, but an unauthorised version eventually came into circulation, so Browne issued a corrected, official version in 1643. By that time, he had moved to Norfolk, married, opened a medical practice, and started a family.

Religio Medici—a work which was eventually placed on the Vatican's *List Of Prohibited Books*—is an intensely personal attempt to reconcile Browne's deeply held religious convictions with a more rational, scientific outlook. Indeed, although Browne generally believed rationality should be subservient to faith, he is often celebrated as an early modern skeptic: a man who challenged accepted beliefs, dogma and misconceptions through careful observation and reasoning. He did this most famously in his next book, *Pseudodoxia Epidemica, or, Enquiries into Very Many Received Tenets and Commonly Presumed Truths* (often simply referred to, more succinctly, as *Vulgar Errors*). In this second work, Browne debunked, amongst other popular notions of the day, the belief that men have one fewer ribs than women, that elephants have no skeletal joints, that hares are hermaphrodites, that male beavers castrate themselves to effect escape from their pursuers, that ostriches can digest iron, and that Jews—the betrayers of Christ—stink to high heaven as divine punishment for the sins of their forefathers. In the same book, according to the *Oxford English Dictionary*, Browne made the first documented use of the word *electricity*. He is also credited with first use of the words *medical, pathology, hallucination, literary*, and *computer*— although not all of them in their modern senses!

Knighted by Charles II, Browne lived a full and respected life, dying on 19th October 1682: his 77th birthday (probably). He was buried in St Peter Mancroft Church in the centre of Norwich.

It would be an extremely satisfying coincidence if Browne's death, like the intolerably dull Shakespeare's, really had fallen on the anniversary of his own birth. The sceptical Browne had once written on the very subject of elderly people dying on their own birthdays. He saw the phenomenon as something astrologers, according to their own claims, should be able, but seldom venture, to predict:

> *Nothing is more common with Infants than to dye on the day of their Nativity, to behold the worldly Hours and but the Fractions thereof; and even to perish before their Nativity in the hidden World of the Womb, and before their good Angel is conceived to undertake them. But in Persons who out-live many Years, and when there are no less than three hundred sixty five days to determine their Lives in every Year; that the first day should make the last, that the Tail of the Snake should return into its Mouth precisely at that time, and they should wind up upon the day of their Nativity, is indeed a remarkable Coincidence, which tho Astrology hath taken witty pains to salve, yet hath it been very wary in making Predictions of it.*

But dying on his own birthday, having written about that very phenomenon, would have been by no means the most remarkable, ironically prophetic coincidence concerning his own death to be found in Browne's writing. For that, we must return to *Urne Burial*, in which he describes one of the benefits of cremation:

To be knav'd out of our graves, to have our skulls made drinking-bowls, and our bones turned into pipes, to delight and sport our enemies, are tragical abominations escaped in burning burials.

In August 1840, while digging a grave for the recently deceased wife of the vicar of St Peter Mancroft Church, a workman, inadvertently or otherwise, dug into Sir Thomas Browne's burial vault. Thom Browne's body lay a-mouldering in the grave, but, as in the case of Adrian's horse, time had spared his epitaph—barely. A brass plaque attached to the coffin still bore the faint Latin inscription: "Hoc Loculo indormiense, Corporis Spagyrici pulvere plumbum in aurum Convertit" ("Sleeping in this Coffin, by the dust of his Alchemical Body, he Converts the lead into gold").

Despite Browne's alchemical epitaph, his lead coffin had remained resolutely leaden, and had pretty much crumbled to dust. While it was being repaired, the church sexton, George Potter, *knav'd* Browne's skull from his grave, giving it to a local chemist, Robert Fitch, for analysis. The pseudoscience of phrenology was all the rage at the time. Fitch arranged for a cast to be made of the skull and returned the original to Potter. But, rather than reburying it, Potter, a man for whose deeds the word *skulduggery* might almost have been invented, secretly sold Browne's skull to a local doctor and amateur antiquarian, Edward Lubbock. In what must surely rate as a *tragical abomination*, Browne's bones were re-interred without his head.

When Lubbock died eight years later, he left Browne's skull to the Norfolk and Norwich Hospital Museum. There it remained for seven decades. After numerous petitions for the return of the stolen skull, the museum finally relented. It was reburied at St Peter Mancroft Church on 4th July 1922, bringing almost to an end the Thomas Browne Affair. Showing a humorous touch for a man of the cloth, the vicar of St Peter Mancroft, Rev. Canon F.J. Meyrick, recorded in the church burial book the re-interment of "The skull of Sir Thomas Browne", writing in the column reserved for the age of the deceased the impressive figure of "317 years". Meyrick made a slight error in his calculation: Sir Thomas Browne's skull was a mere 316 years old at the time—just shy of one-third of a Methuselah.

How much more ancient than Thomas Browne's skull must the cremated human remains in this urnfield be? Assuming any of them have survived the ravages of time, that is. Calderdale's *Register of Ancient Monuments* confidently states the site "will retain cremation burials", explaining that excavations in 1897 produced burnt human bone and fragments of prehistoric pottery. A 1933 excavation of the *hub* on which I'm now standing unearthed half a quern, presumably made from the local millstone grit. The *Register* also explains that such urnfields usually comprise a ditch or bank within a stone circle, with a mound or standing stone sometimes at the centre. So perhaps my Stonehenge comparison isn't so fanciful after all. Perhaps there was once a circle of stones associated with this urnfield which were later moved elsewhere. The relocated prehistoric standing stone known as *Churn Milk Joan*, silhouetted on the eastern skyline just a few hundred metres away, springs immediately to mind.

There you go again, Richard, conjuring up hypotheses based on little or no evidence. There aren't any stones, so they must have been moved. Just listen to yourself!

Do we know anything for certain about the people who built this urnfield? Did the *iniquity of oblivion* spare any of their culture, beyond the odd potsherd? One thing is for sure: the people who made this urnfield weren't English. The English wouldn't arrive in these islands for many hundreds of years. The prevailing view seems to be that these urnfields are associated with the emergence of Celtic culture in the late Bronze Age, three-thousand or more years ago—three or four *Methuselahs*, according to Sir Thomas Browne's unconventional scale of antiquity. That's far too early for written records in Britain, but what about the oral tradition? Could anything have survived?

Charles Darwin might not have much to say on the subject of literary criticism, but he does express views on the classification of languages. In *On the Origin of Species*, he explains how the relationships between languages, like those between species, must be genealogical in nature. He goes on to hypothesise that the family tree of languages must closely reflect the family tree of the different races of mankind that speak them:

> *If we possessed a perfect pedigree of mankind, a genealogical arrangement of the races of man would afford the best classification of the various languages now spoken throughout the world; and if all extinct languages, and all intermediate and slowly changing dialects, had to be included, such an arrangement would, I think, be the only possible one. Yet it might be that some very ancient language had altered little, and had given rise to few new languages, whilst others (owing to the spreading and subsequent isolation and states of civilisation of the several races, descended from a common race) had altered much, and had given rise to many new languages and dialects. The various degrees of difference in the languages from the same stock, would have to be expressed by groups subordinate to groups; but the proper or even only possible arrangement would still be genealogical; and this would be strictly natural, as it would connect together all languages, extinct and modern, by the closest affinities, and would give the filiation and origin of each tongue.*

Darwin, as usual, is pretty much on the ball. The family tree of languages does indeed closely reflect human history, albeit with one or two anomalies. Nobody, for example, seems to have a blind clue where the Basque language fits in: it bears no known relationship with any other tongue. But not so the various Celtic languages. These are thought to have descended from an aboriginal *Proto-Celtic* language, and can be arranged into the two broad branches of the Celtic family tree: the so-called *Q-Celtic* and *P-Celtic* groups. *Proto-Celtic* is believed to have contained numerous words which began with a *kw-* sound. This sound, depending on the word in question, was either retained or became a *k-* in the *Q-Celtic* group, but evolved into a *p-* sound in the *P-Celtic* group. There are several other sets of consistent sound-changes differentiating the two groups. So, for example, it's assumed the *Proto-Celtic* word for 'head' must have sounded something like *kwennos*. In the *P-Celtic* group of languages, the *kw-* changed to a *p-*, eventually becoming *pen* in Welsh, and *penn* in Cornish. In *Q-Celtic*, the *kw-* changed to a *k-*, becoming *ceann* in Irish and Scots' Gaelic.

Whether or not the original Celts in Britain spoke a *P-Celtic* or *Q-Celtic* language, or whether they still spoke *Proto-Celtic*, is a hotly debated subject which need not detain us. But it suffices to say that a modern-day Welsh-, Cornish-, Breton-, Irish-, Scots' Gaelic- or Manx-speaker would stand a far better chance of being able to communicate verbally (to some extent at least) with the people who made this Yorkshire urnfield, than most of the monolingual Anglophones, myself included, who now live around here.

And, yes, it turns out the people who build this urnfield did indeed leave a linguistic legacy—albeit, most likely, by way of their Romano-British descendants. Small snippets of their ancient language still survive, unnoticed and almost forgotten, in a few local place names: in the *pen-* syllable, for example, of the doubly tautological, tri-lingual Pendle Hill (literal translation: *Hill-hill Hill*); and in the Celtic name for the *swift-stream* down in the valley, our lovely River Calder.

The people buried in this urnfield left a record. Small linguistic elements of their culture escaped oblivion. Their epitaphs survive in the names of rivers, fields and hills. You can still read them on maps; you can still hear them talked about in the local pubs—even though you might not realise it.

The fight goes on. The iniquity of oblivion has not scattered all of her poppies. Entropy's victory is not complete.

Not yet.

In the Clouds

What on earth possessed me to come up here in this weather?

I knew exactly what it would be like: I drove through it on my way over the tops to Halifax this morning. Wet, foggy and miserable. Washed-out, monochrome clouds drifting low over the valley, wetter than wet. Real watercolour clouds, blotched, bleeding down into grey. Pennine clouds.

On the paved track through the bog, everything— the grass, the heather, the very air—has a drenched freshness to it. Seeping banks of mist have turned cobwebs into necklaces, grass seed-heads into tiaras. The world is crisp, expectant, eerily still.

As soon as I turn up the hill, the mist folds in. I don't even see it coming. All of a sudden, I'm in cloud. Fat water-drops condense out of hyper-saturated air, pattering randomly on my jacket and hood. Precipitation, but not quite rain. My beard beads. Everything is colourless, sodden, claustrophobic. The universe is a fifty-metre-radius hemisphere, with me at its centre. No sound encroaches. There's no sky, no horizon. Just me and rock and heather, shrouded in wetness.

It is utterly exhilarating.

I forget just how invigorating it can be to walk on the Moor in lousy weather. It's almost as if something in my perverse subconscious doesn't want me to go out and get drenched. But I'm never disappointed, if I get off my fat arse and venture up here.

I reach the top and follow the track to the trig point. Some colour has returned. The heather up here is in full flower, purple fading into fog, but the view has been stolen. It's 12th August—the so-called *Glorious Twelfth*—but the grouse will be safe for one more day at least. Noble tradition notwithstanding, it would be plain irresponsible to be firing off shotguns in such poor visibility.

I touch the trig point to make it official and head north along the invisible edge. The track meanders through the heather, dipping and rising. It's a good job I know where I am, as there are no features for me to calibrate my bearings. It's impossible to walk in gently undulating hill-country in fog like this without being reminded of Tolkien's Barrow Downs and their blood-chilling inhabitants, the barrow-wights. In this case, the reminder is enhanced by knowledge of the ancient burial cairn, *Miller's Grave*, just a couple of hundred metres or so over the brow of the hill. But I shan't be passing that way today, unless, like Frodo and his companions, I become hopelessly lost. I mustn't be complacent, though. To my considerable embarrassment, I did once wander off course up here in dense fog, only to be re-orientated ten minutes later by the bells of Heptonstall church chiming across the valley, from what seemed very much the wrong direction.

I pause by the convenient rock. I often sit here to take in the view, sometimes with a flask of tea. But there's no view to take in today, even though the fog has thinned. I'm about to continue, when a ghostly silhouette emerges from the mist, flying almost directly towards me. A crow, I guess, judging by its size. But, no, far better than any crow: a young peregrine—a female—flying with slow, methodical wing-beats low across the heather. Her rounded head is tucked into her broad shoulders, hunched against the drizzle. She must have seen me, but doesn't alter her course, which will bring her within ten metres of me.

I've never been so close to a wild peregrine before. She's magnificent. Sleek, powerful, long wings, huge yellow talons. The perfect killing machine.

Oliver Goldsmith's phrase *she stoops to conquer* could have been coined to describe the peregrine's mode of attack. She preys on other birds—pigeons, waders, grouse, anything of a reasonable size—flying high to seek victims through her predatory, front-facing, stereoscopic eyes. As with our own eyes, the peregrine's have a tiny pit located near the centre of the retina, the fovea, packed with special cone-shaped photo-receptors to provide high-definition central vision. Unlike our own eyes, though, the peregrine's contain a second fovea, slightly offset towards the beak. This has even more photo-receptors, giving the peregrine five times our visual acuity. This, incidentally, makes a mockery of the tired, anti-evolutionist taunt, "What good is half an eye?" From a peregrine's point of view, we only have one-fifth of an eye, but it serves us well enough.

To prevent facial glare interfering with her vision, the peregrine has also evolved a dark stripe beneath her eyes: her so-called *moustache*. It's a solution arrived at independently by other fast-moving predators, such as cheetahs and American football players.

Having singled out her prey far below, the peregrine adjusts her orientation, spills air from her wings, and enters into a dive—her legendary *stoop*. She flaps her wings at first to gain speed more quickly, then tucks them in to minimise air resistance, letting gravity take over. Her profile becomes streamlined, teardrop-shaped. She plummets. Here, she is presented with a dilemma. To make best use of her second, super-definition fovea for as long as possible, she needs to keep her target slightly to the corner of her eye. But, if she turns her head to achieve this, she'll become less streamlined, introducing drag. Nature has endowed her with a pragmatic solution. Instead of plunging straight at her target, she spins towards it in an ever-decreasing spiral.

Nobody is entirely sure at what speed the peregrine's stoop maxes out. She typically reaches speeds of over 200 miles per hour, making her the fastest creature on the planet. Moving at such incredible speed presents the peregrine with additional problems, not least, how to breathe. She has evolved cone-shaped baffles in her nostrils to redirect and slow the air entering them. Jet engines have adopted a similar design for the same purpose. Hurtling down through the atmosphere at such speed also creates problems for the peregrine's eyes. They could easily dry out, or be damaged by particles in the air. She protects her eyes during the stoop with her *nictitating membranes*: transparent third eyelids, drawn across the eyes like fighter pilots' visors.

As the peregrine bears down on her prey, her lethal talons swing forward to rip flesh, disembowel, and occasionally decapitate. As with all collisions, sheer momentum is a major factor in the damage done. But the stoop doesn't always result in a kill. The falcon often misses her quarry. Natural Selection has honed the peregrine for predation, but it has also honed her prey to see her coming and take evasive action. Every new stoop heralds the latest skirmish in a ruthless evolutionary arms-race.

I can't get over her size. It might seem strange to us primates, but female peregrines—correctly known as *falcons*—are noticeably larger than the male *tiercels*. The *Oxford English Dictionary* explains that the name *tiercel* (also spelt *tercel*) is based on the Latin word *tertius*, meaning 'third'—perhaps from the unfounded belief that male birds hatched from the third egg in the clutch, thereby supposedly explaining their smaller size. In his 1967 classic, *The Peregrine*, J.A. Baker suggests that this sexual dimorphism might, to some extent, prevent mating pairs of peregrines from competing for the same food resources: tiercels will tend to hunt smaller prey than falcons. Furthermore, preying on different species could improve the two sexes' chances of catching food for their young. Spreading their bets, so to speak.

Even allowing for my peregrine's being female, she seems larger than I would have expected. I later learn that I'm not the first to notice how birds of prey can look bigger in the mist. In her wonderful 1977 book, *The Living Mountain*, Nan Shepherd describes a similar foggy encounter with a surprisingly large peregrine. She quotes some draft lines from the poet Gerard Manley Hopkins:

[I...] *Must see the eagle's bulk, render'd in mists, Hang of a treble size.*

But the unabashed, hideously unpoetic sceptic in me realises that, in order to see a bird of prey through a thick mist, one must, almost by definition, be closer to it than normal, so it's bound to look bigger. Indeed, today's poor visibility is probably the only reason I'm seeing this magnificent creature in the first place: peregrines' visual acuity might be five times better than our own, but, in such poor visibility, the falcon's eyesight is no better than mine. She's been forced to fly low to stand any chance of spotting her prey.

The peregrine beats slowly, confidently past. I'm

having an adrenaline rush. I've never seen such a magnificent, graceful animal.

And then I remember that I have:

Mid-winter, ten or more years ago. I'd recently joined a gym as part of a not-for-the-first-time, soon-to-be-abandoned new year's resolution to get fit. On this particular morning, I couldn't help noticing a young woman in her early twenties running pretty much flat-out on one of the treadmills. I'm no expert, but I would say she was one gear down from a full sprint—an 800 metres' pace. She made it look effortless.

An hour and a half later, as I left the gym showered and nauseous, the young woman was still running. She hadn't slackened her pace once. She was cruising along at the same ridiculous speed. There was no jarring or swaying, not a hint of fatigue, she just ran, and ran, and ran. It was the most natural, graceful movement I'd ever seen performed by a human being.

For all I know, she's still running.

We *Homo sapiens* are a remarkable and talented species. Our massive brains set us apart from the rest of the animal kingdom. They enable us to do astonishing things. I've stood on the Great Wall of China. I've gazed in awe at Durham Cathedral, the domed roof of the Pantheon, and the ceiling of the Sistine Chapel. I've stood at our gate and waved at the International Space Station as it passed overhead with Mike, my friend Karen's friend, on board. And yet, watching that young woman run reminded me that we came out of the African savannah only yesterday. That, until recently, we were all hunter-gatherers who needed to travel great distances quickly on foot in search of meat. It reminded me, above all else, that the Boss was right: chimps like us, baby, we were born to run.

To any impartial observer, the family resemblance between us humans and our nearest living relatives, the chimpanzees and bonobos, must seem uncanny. Yet there are one or two important differences. Many of these differences are down to our different lifestyles. Others were almost certainly contributing factors towards those different lifestyles. Others, no doubt, are a combination of the two. Natural Selection is an iterative process, and it never lets up.

You look at chimpanzees, and you look at us. There are obvious physical differences. We have longer legs, giving us longer strides. We have longer waists, enabling our bodies to twist, counterbalancing our legs. We have shorter body-hair, and we sweat, allowing us to lose excess heat through our skin. We have magnificent buttocks, allowing us to move our legs quickly. All of these features, and more beside, show that we have put our tree-dwelling days well and truly behind us. Our bodies evolved for running.

Well, some of our bodies, at least.

As the falcon heads away, her flight turns into a glide. She descends slowly, landing behind a clump of heather one-hundred metres away. I've no idea what she's up to.

My camera is in my bag for protection against the wet. I take it out and move towards where the bird landed. If I'm lucky, I might be able to grab a photo or two. But she's watching me. I've walked no more than ten paces when she rises from the heather, and disappears into the fog, accompanied by half a dozen half-hearted camera clicks. The photos will be dreadful, but I don't care. I return to the track, elated at my unexpected encounter with this impeccable creature.

The most recent common ancestor of the peregrine falcon and the woman running in the gym—that is, the most recent common ancestor of birds and mammals, and of all the dinosaurs (of which birds are the sole surviving branch), and of tortoises and turtles, snakes and lizards, alligators and crocodiles—lived around 310 million years ago, as the millstone grit of the Moor was being deposited in equatorial river deltas, and the coal measures were being formed. This noble creature, like all its surviving descendants, lived alongside millions of other equally noble species on a diverse and thriving planet. Even if, in the vanishingly unlikely event that its fossil has survived the iniquity of oblivion, and some lucky palaeontologist were to dig it up, we wouldn't be able to say for certain that we were looking at our long-lost common ancestor, rather than some unlucky close relative whose dead-end line didn't lead to us, the birds, and the tortoises. Yet we can say what this creature would have looked like. It would have had four limbs, set in the side of its body rather than underneath, each terminated with five digits. It would have had a tail, a snout, and a lower jaw containing articular and quadrate bones. In other words, it would have looked like a lizard. We can also say that our common ancestor laid eggs which contained an internal amniotic membrane. Which, incidentally, answers the hoary old question about the chicken and the egg: the egg came first.

We can confidently say such things about our most recent common ancestor because its diverse descendants alive on the planet today still mostly have these characteristics. Snakes have no limbs. We mammals have no articular and quadrate bones in our jaws, and, with the exception of echidnas and platypuses, don't lay eggs. Birds have only four digits hidden inside their wings, and two to four toes on their feet. But, if you look more closely at these descendants—especially if you look at their developing embryos or their DNA—you can usually find some remnant of the ancestral form still in there. The skeletons of some snakes, such as boas and pythons, still bear useless remnants of a pelvis. Mammals' articular and quadrate bones move away from the lower jaw in the developing embryo and become the tiny malleus and incus—*hammer* and *anvil*—bones of the inner-ear. Early on in their development, chicken embryos have a full hand of five digits in their wings, but one of these digits is reabsorbed and isn't found in the fully developed bird.

Going farther back in time, before the most recent common ancestor of birds and mammals, the lineages are merged. It's common ancestors all the way back from there. Go back 340 million years, give or take, and you'll reach the first tetrapod—the first creature with four limbs—which probably also had five digits per limb, and most likely lived in swamps. As well as us, that creature's descendants include the amphibians. Go back a further 100 million years, and you'll reach the first animal with a bony skeleton. That creature lived in the oceans. It was, without putting too fine a point on it, a fish.

Evolution by means of Natural Selection is an incredibly creative process. It can transform a fish into a falcon, a tree-dwelling ape into a long-distance runner. Yet it's a messy, inefficient process. Evolution doesn't have a free hand. It can never start from scratch. It can only tinker with what's already there.

I was wrong to describe the peregrine as *the perfect killing machine*. Even she is compromised by her ancestry. Like all other species, she comes laden with historical baggage. If you were to sit down with a blank piece of paper and try to design the ultimate aerial killing machine, unconstrained by biological history, you wouldn't come up with a peregrine falcon. Doesn't stooping at 200 miles per hour and colliding with one's prey seem an incredibly dangerous and inefficient way to catch lunch? Wouldn't some sort of air-to-air missile be less risky, and more effective? Yes, the suggestion is ridiculous: Darwin showed us that's not how new species are made. But there are still those who would have you believe that the peregrine falcon, and every other species on this planet, was indeed constructed from scratch, by an intelligent, omnipotent designer who needn't have been constrained in any way. If you ever have the misfortune to end up in conversation with anyone who believes such nonsense, as I often do, ask them to explain the peregrine's inexplicable lack of air-to-air missiles. That should shut them up. Not that it will.

We humans are also constrained by ancestry, and that ancestry is written into our bodies. As Charles Darwin wrote in the final paragraph of *The Descent of Man*:

> *Man may be excused for feeling some pride at having risen, though not through his own exertions, to the very summit of the organic scale; and the fact of his having thus risen, instead of having been aboriginally placed there, may give him hopes for a still higher destiny in the distant future. But we are not here concerned with hopes or fears, only with the truth as far as our reason allows us to discover it. I have given the evidence to the best of my ability; and we must acknowledge, as it seems to me, that man with all his noble qualities, with sympathy which feels for the most debased, with benevolence which extends not only to other men but to the humblest living creature, with his god-like intellect which has penetrated into the movements and constitution of the solar system—with all these exalted powers—Man still bears in his bodily frame the indelible stamp of his lowly origin.*

As does Woman:

For all her elegance, the running woman's four limbs—the legs and arms she used so effectively for running—were inherited from a lizard-like ancestor which moved with its belly near the ground. Her beautifully adapted skeleton was inherited from a fish. In fact, depending on how you define a fish, you could argue that the young woman running so gracefully on that treadmill was, quite literally, a glorified fish out of water. The blood that coursed through her veins was modified fish-blood. The lungs that replenished her fish-blood with oxygen were modified oesophageal pouches that allowed her fish ancestors to gulp air when oxygen was in short supply. The heart that pumped the re-oxygenated fish-blood around her body was a modified fish-heart.

Go to a mirror and look yourself in the eye. No, move closer. Look carefully. Use your fingers to hold your eyelids back if you need to. Look at the ball of each eye, right next to the tear-duct. Do you see it? Do you see that tiny transparent flap running top to bottom? That's your *plica semilunaris*. It's all that's left of your *nictitating membrane*: the transparent third eyelid that you and the peregrine inherited from some ancient common ancestor. An indelible stamp of your lowly origin.

You, me, the running woman, the peregrine—our cousins, the chimps, the boa constrictors, T-rexes, and natterjack toads—none of us was designed from scratch by some intelligent designer. We got here the hard way: Darwin's way. And it shows. We still bear the signs in our bodily frames. None of us is perfect. Every single one of us is a glorious, kludgy compromise.

Vestiges of our animal ancestry live on in our bodies,

as vestiges of our cultural legacy live on in our languages and local place names. The clues are there, if you open your modified fish-eyes, and make best use of your modified fish-brain.

Anyone who thinks this view of life somehow *belittles* the glories of Nature needs to have their modified ganglion nerve-clumps seen to. How much more noble to be part of a multi-billion-year, ever-evolving lineage of magnificent kludges—a lineage which ultimately unites us with every other living organism on the planet—than the unchanged offspring of a single act of creation by an imaginary designer a mere 6,000 years ago!

I head over the final rise, and drop down again on the far side, taking the left fork in the track. The fog is less dense over here. I'm still on a high.

What's that?!

To my delight, the peregrine re-emerges from the mist, gliding across my line of sight. She swoops down and lands on top of a low cairn a hundred metres away. She looks about, then fixes her super-definition gaze on me. So, this is how a grouse feels.

Time to try my luck once more. I pull out my camera, and advance slowly towards the falcon, clicking away. The fog, though thinning, is still thick. I know the photos will be terrible, but I have to try.

Then, something distracts her. The peregrine's head rotates to her left. Following her gaze, I see some other idiot is out on the Moor in this dreadful weather: a man walking his dog. The falcon takes to the air, flying slowly back the way she came. The last I see of her is as she glides in another long, low descent, disappearing behind the rise of the hill.

I turn for home, having made a not-for-the-first-time, soon-to-be-abandoned resolution to get off my fat arse and walk on the Moor in atrocious weather more often.

White-arse

Down the long slope to the corner where the top field edges into the Moor. A favourite spot to take in the view towards Stoodley Pike. The monument is looking as monumental as ever this afternoon, standing proud on the skyline. *Phallic*, some would call it. Poor bastards. I'm glad mine isn't that shape!

I could turn left here and follow the wall back towards the golf course, or I could carry straight on, alongside the other wall, towards the grouse-shooters' hut. It's August, hot and sunny, with a strong, cooling wind from the south. Perfect. Of course I'll take the longer route. Straight on it is!

I often spook a few rabbits around here. There are burrows in the field over the wall, and on the slopes of Tom Tittiman, the hill to my right. I reckon there must be a burrow entrance beneath the hut as well: rabbits tend to bolt under there as I approach. But there's no sign of any rabbits today; just a few indignant meadow pipits being buffeted by wind.

I look south. You can see our house from here, if you

look carefully. It's amazing how well it blends into the landscape. Mind you, it is made out of the local millstone grit. Pretty good camouflage.

I'm about to continue, when I spot a white flash out of the corner of my eye. Sneaky: a rabbit has waited until I was looking the other way before making a break for it. There it is again, flitting through the tufts of moor-grass. But no, I'm mistaken: that's no rabbit's scut; that's the bobbing white rump of a wheatear. Fabulous! Wheatears are always a treat.

If I were ever crass enough to draw up a top-ten list of favourite birds, wheatears—or *northern wheatears*, as we're supposed to refer to them these days—would certainly be on it. They bring good vibes, having fond associations. If I see a wheatear, I'm usually somewhere I love: on a headland in Anglesey, or amongst limestone outcrops in the Yorkshire Dales, but most likely on the Moor. Wheatears like hanging out in the same sorts of places as I do. But they would earn their place on my hypothetical top-ten list in their own right. They're such elegant birds; outrageous flirts, whose curiosity about humans brings them close, but whose wariness means they never get *too* close. Wheatears like to tease.

The bird whisks from beneath a clump of heather and lands on the wall just beyond the hut, about fifteen metres in front of me. A female, by the look of it, or possibly a juvenile male. I'm holding out for female. At this time of year, they're difficult to tell apart, both sporting light brown upper feathers, rather than the mature males' blue-grey, and both lacking the latter's dark eye-stripe. Her under-feathers are a beautiful, slightly salmony buff. The word *dapper* springs to mind. Wheatears always look impeccably neat; *formal* somehow. Bigger but leaner than a robin, smaller than a thrush, they have a certain poise that singles them out from other birds. That, and their outrageous white backsides.

I remember my first ever wheatear encounter. It was May 1977. I was twelve years old. My parents had taken my sister and me for a coastal walk at Thurstaston Country Park, a few miles from our home on the Wirral Peninsula. We were just returning to the car along the cliff top, when Mum spotted a pair of wheatears on a grassy bank hunting insects. She was terrifically excited: she hadn't seen a wheatear for years. She explained that the bird was called a *wheat-ear* because it had a light stripe, like an eyebrow, running across its temple and down towards the back of its head. Some people, she said, thought this stripe, which I later learned was called a *supercilium*, looked like an ear of wheat tucked behind the bird's own ear. I was ecstatic: a wheatear was worth 25 points in my *I-Spy Birds* book, in which I recorded the sighting for posterity (originally in pencil, later gone over in blue ballpoint to make it official). In my excitement, I mistakenly recorded the location as Thurstaston Common, an area of gorse-covered heathland half a mile down the road—or *Thurthaston common*, as I spelt it.

Wheatear (34) An active, restless little ground-living bird, about the size of a sparrow. Watch for the white rump on both male and female, and for the white side feathers in their tails. While breeding the male has a blue-grey back and a broad white eye-stripe. In autumn he looks like the female: buff with a brownish back. Migrant.

I-SPYed (34) at............

Thurthaston common

May 14.77 Score **25**

34

It wasn't until many years later that I learnt where wheatears *really* got their name. It's on account of their distinctive white rumps: *wheat-ears* is a corruption of the Old English *hwit-oers*, meaning 'white-arse'! Over the years, prudes had invented various fake etymologies to explain the name, of which Mum's was just one. Not that Mum was in any way a prude; she just told me what she'd been told. In such ways are myths made. When, many years later, I informed Mum of the true derivation of the bird's name, she pretended to be shocked, but was secretly delighted.

The wheatear's official scientific name, *Oenanthe oenanthe*, as chosen by none other than the inventor of the binomial naming system, Carl Linnaeus, is also somewhat obscure, although perhaps more poetic. It derives from the Greek *ainos*, meaning 'wine', and *anthos*, meaning 'flower', supposedly referring to the wheatear's annual return to Greece just as the grapevines are blossoming.

The wheatear is suddenly joined on the wall by two others. They take turns dropping down to the ground, snatching up insects, then returning to the wall. I could watch them all day. Such energetic, aristocratic birds in their buff dinner-suits. I edge closer. They humour then taunt me, allowing me to come close, but not close enough to take a decent photo, before they flit ahead along the wall. It's a game we've played many times: I continue to edge closer, they continue to maintain a respectable distance. In Anglesey last summer, similarly taunted by wheatears, I tried a different approach, choosing a convenient rock and sitting down, waiting to see what would happen. Eventually, curiosity got the better of them, and they sidled close enough for me to take some half-decent shots. But there's nowhere to sit up here, so I keep edging closer, and the wheatears keep flitting away.

The wheatear's seasonal migration is one of the wonders of the natural world. They spend our winter in central Africa, but migrate north and east as far as Siberia and Alaska, and north and west as far as Greenland and eastern Canada. In the latter case, no passerine (the large order of perching birds, which includes all songbirds) is thought to migrate farther over water. In the summer breeding season, therefore, wheatears are distributed over a vast swathe of the northern hemisphere, covering much of northern Eurasia and parts of North America, as well as Greenland and Iceland. But they all converge back in central Africa for the winter.

In his book *Bird Migration*, Ian Newton points out that it would make far more sense for the Siberian and Alaskan wheatears to migrate to Southeast Asia or Central America for the winter, rather than travelling the far greater distance to Africa. Similarly, on the opposite side of the North American landmass, it would also be much easier for the eastern Canadian birds to migrate to Central America. Newton suggests that these birds' inefficient and risky migration routes are likely to be the result of historical and evolutionary constraints. The wheatear's northern range, he argues, gradually spread as the glaciers retreated after the last glacial maximum, making their migration routes progressively longer. To change to a shorter, easier route now, however, would require the Siberian, Alaskan and eastern Canadian birds to migrate south in very different directions from at present. Such a change would be too great an evolutionary leap to make in one fell swoop. A series of smaller, incremental changes would also be problematical, as any intermediate routes would lead the birds over thousands of miles of empty ocean. The wheatears are, therefore, constrained by their evolutionary history. They stick to their inefficient migration routes because those routes made sense in the past. To change them now would require the wheatear to evolve a totally different migration strategy. But evolution through Natural Selection doesn't work that way; it can only tinker with what's already there. Species come laden with historical baggage. Memories of the last glacial maximum survive in the wheatear's genes.

Scientists have only recently established beyond doubt that wheatears do indeed migrate all the way from North America to central Africa. Isotope analyses of winter-grown feathers taken from birds in their summer breeding grounds indicated that eastern Canadian wheatears overwinter in western Africa, while Alaskan wheatears overwinter in eastern Africa. These findings were later confirmed when small tracking devices were attached to 46 birds in their North American breeding grounds, four of which were retrieved the following summer. Three devices were retrieved from wheatears that bred in Alaska. These indicated that the birds had migrated to eastern Africa via northern Russia, Kazakhstan, and the Arabian Desert. The single device retrieved from the wheatears that bred in eastern Canada indicated that the bird in question had crossed the northern Atlantic Ocean to the British Isles in just four days, via Baffin Island and possibly the southern tip of Greenland. It had then turned south, crossing Europe, to overwinter near the Mauritanian coast in western Africa. All four birds had subsequently followed similar migration routes back to their summer breeding grounds. All this by a little bird weighing just 25g, burdened with a 1.4g tracking device. One further reason, if any were needed, for keeping wheatears in my top ten.

The wheatears that breed on the Moor have a reasonably sensible migration route by comparison. They and their offspring will head for sub-Saharan Africa in late August or early September. Any birds I see on the Moor after then are likely to be passage migrants travelling from Iceland or Greenland. Although still recognised as the same species, the Greenland race of wheatears is slightly larger than those that breed in Britain. This demonstrates a phenomenon known as *Bergmann's Rule*. In the nineteenth century, the German anatomist Christian Bergmann established that warm-blooded species living in colder environments tend to be larger than their counterparts living in warmer environments. This is because larger animals are better at retaining heat than smaller ones. An animal twice as big as another in all directions will have four times the surface area, but eight times the volume. Body heat is stored throughout an animal's body (i.e. its volume), but is lost through the animal's skin (i.e. its surface area). The bigger animal in our example has a volume-to-surface-area ratio twice as big ($8 \div 4 = 2$) as the smaller animal, so will retain heat twice as effectively. As a result, throughout the world, warm-blooded species have evolved to become bigger in colder climates. As Greenland is colder than Britain, its wheatears are larger than ours.

Larger wheatears will have more meat on them, I suppose. I can't imagine eating one, but people used to.

They're very tasty, by all accounts, although a little on the stingy side. You'd feel hard done by if you only ended up with a drumstick.

In his *Curious and Diverting Journies, Thro' the Whole Island of Great-Britain* (1724–27), Daniel Defoe recorded that:

> *they have from the South-Downs, the bird call'd a wheatear, or as we may call them, the English ortolans, the most delicious taste for a creature of one mouthful, for 'tis little more, that can be imagin'd; but these are very dear at Tunbridge, they are much cheaper at Seaford, Lewis, and that side of the country.*

Defoe's contemporary, Jonathan Swift, in his *Directions to Servants* (1731), offered the cook some practical advice on how to save time roasting wheatears and other small birds:

> *Good Cooks cannot abide what they justly call fidling Work, where Abundance of Time is spent and little done: Such, for Instance, is the dressing small Birds, requiring a world of Cookery and Clutter, and a second or third Spit, which by the Way is absolutely needless; for it will be a very ridiculous Thing indeed, if a Spit which is strong enough to turn a Sirloyn of Beef, should not be able to turn a Lark; however, if your Lady be nice, and is afraid that a large Spit will tear them, place them handsomely in the Dripping-pan, where the Fat of roasted Mutton or Beef falling on the Birds; will serve to baste them, and so save both Time and Butter; for what Cook of any Spirit would lose her Time in picking Larks, Wheat-ears, and other small Birds; therefore, if you cannot get the Maids, or the young Misses to assist you, e'en make short Work, and either singe or*

flay them; there is no great Loss in the Skins, and the Flesh is just the same.

In his 1789 masterpiece, *The Natural History of Selbourne*, Britain's most celebrated early naturalist, the Rev. Gilbert White, described the trapping of wheatears, after briefly discussing the mystery of their migration:

> *Mr. Stillingfleet, in his Tracts, says that, "if the wheatear (œnanthe) does not quit England, it certainly shifts places; for about harvest they are not to be found, where there was before great plenty of them." This well accounts for the vast quantities that are caught about that time on the south downs near Lewes, where they are esteemed a delicacy. There have been shepherds, I have been credibly informed, that have made many pounds in a season by catching them in traps. And though such multitudes are taken, I never saw (and I am well acquainted with those parts) above two or three at a time: for they are never gregarious. They may perhaps migrate in general; and, for that purpose, draw towards the coast of Sussex in Autumn: but that they do not all withdraw I am sure; because I see a few stragglers in many counties, at all times of the year, especially about warrens and stone quarries.*

Wheatears were, it turned out, remarkably easy to catch. As a result, they were eaten in great abundance. All it took to trap one was a shallow trench, some turf, and a small snare. The process was described by W.H. Hudson, one of the founders of *The Royal Society for the Protection of Birds*, in his 1900 book, *Nature in Downland*:

In July the shepherds made their "coops", as their traps were called—a T-shaped trench about fourteen inches long, over which the two long narrow sods cut neatly out of the turf were adjusted, grass downwards. A small opening was left at the end for ingress, and there was room in the passage for the bird to pass through toward the chinks of light coming from the two ends of the cross passage. At the inner end of the passage a horse-hair springe was set, by which the bird was caught by the neck as it passed in, but the noose did not as a rule strangle the bird.

Thankfully, by the time of Hudson's writing, the practice of ensnaring wheatears had been banned, although it continues to this day, illegally, in certain countries in and around the Mediterranean.

Having decided that I seem harmless enough, the wheatears fly down from their wall and land at the side of the track a short distance in front of me. They stare intently into the tussocky grass and heather, occasionally darting in after insects. As ever, though, they continue to maintain a safe distance as I advance slowly towards them.

Why the white arses, I wonder? The trouble with such distinctive features is that they cry out for evolutionary explanations. The great American palaeontologist, evolutionary biologist, and essayist Stephen Jay Gould coined the term evolutionary Just-So stories to describe plausible hypotheses conjured up out of thin air to explain the advantages of particular biological features. But it's OK to hypothesise: as-yet untested hypotheses are one of the building blocks of science. And conjuring up specious evolutionary Just-So stories can be great fun. Anyone can play:

Off the top of my head, I can think of several 'explanations' for the wheatear's characteristic backside. For example, in flight, the bobbing white rump might distract predators. Experiments have shown that peregrine falcons seem to find it more difficult to catch white-rumped pigeons. But surely the white rumps also risk attracting the attention of predators in the first place! Besides, the wheatear's preferred tactics for avoiding predators are either to hide, or to freeze motionless for several minutes. In these cases, the white rump would either be irrelevant or remain a hindrance. So perhaps it's a Sexual Selection thing. Perhaps female wheatears find white rumps a turn-on. Or they might just be a convenient way for the birds to spot members of their own species—to separate the wheatears from the chaffinches, so to speak. Or something else entirely. That's the problem with evolutionary Just-So stories: Charles Darwin, gave us such a powerful way to look at Nature that we're sometimes spoilt for choice between equally plausible explanations. Until we put them to the test, that is. I'm sure it must be possible to devise experiments to test my various hypotheses to explain the wheatear's white rump, but I'm equally sure that scientists must have more pressing matters to attend to— although I would also have said the same about tracking wheatears' migration routes. Even if they did carry out such experiments, I shouldn't be at all surprised if the results proved inconclusive. Who says that any feature of an organism need only have just one use? Perhaps there's an element of truth in all of my Just-So stories!

The moor gate approaches. Realising that they're about to run out of track, the wheatears take off and head back the way they came. They disappear over the wall in a triple-flash of white arses. I watch them depart with a huge grin on my face. Any day that involves wheatears is, by definition, *a good day*.

I glance at my watch. Home and a late lunch beckon. Seeing all these wheatears has made me feel rather peckish.

Trig Point

I reach the top of the slope and pause to catch my breath... Nearly there!

Skirting the hilltop quarries, I follow the narrow path. The trig point rises from the heather, gleaming white against graphite sky. Even without the path, I would be drawn towards it, the only other vertical around here: a square-based concrete pillar, four feet tall, tapering slightly, truncated by a flat top.

Trig points hold a strange fascination for me. As a child, I used to think they marked the official summits of hills. I still do. If there's a trig point near the top, you can't claim to have climbed a hill until you've touched it—even if the trig point isn't at the actual summit. A trig point is an unequivocal destination. Climbing a hill and not touching the trig point would be like going to Rome and not visiting the Pantheon: you've come all that way, it would be perverse not to. So, as custom dictates, I touch the concrete block, and check the number on its *flush bracket*: the whitewashed brass plaque set into its base. It's a number I know by heart: S4643, the trig point's official benchmark designation.

How many times have I touched this trig point? It must be well into the hundreds by now. I've been up here in all weathers: wind, rain, fog, ice, snow, and sunshine. Yes, we do occasionally get sunshine. The seasons change, the weather changes, but the trig point remains constant. Solid and dependable. Right where you left it. Which is the whole point of trig points, come to think of it.

I turn, as ever, to take in the view. You always get good views from trig points. That's why they built them where they did. You need to be able to see lots of other places from them, so it makes sense to build them in places with good views. And this view really is a belter!

I always start my 360° panoramic sweep just west of south, where the perfectly named Blackstone Edge broods amongst pylons on the horizon. *Blackstone Edge*: how Brontë is that? How come there isn't a folk reel named in its honour? Perhaps there is. The name says it all: an edge marked by an outcrop of black millstone grit. Standing high above the lands to the west, it defines the western edge of this section of the Pennines. The best cloud-sea I ever saw was from Blackstone Edge, looking west into the sunset across the fog-covered lowlands of Greater Manchester, Cheshire and Merseyside. The view across the horizon-wide fog was breathtaking. Any fog in the area is usually found on top of Blackstone Edge, near the reservoir, as the moisture-laden prevailing winds are forced up over the edge and cooled. But, on that day, there were no winds, and the fog was confined to the lowlands. The crimson clouds went on forever. On clear days, you can see Snowdon from Blackstone Edge: a view across three counties of Northern England and pretty much the whole of North Wales. On days like those, physical geography suddenly makes complete sense, and the very idea of county and national boundaries seems absurd. Which it is, when you think about it.

Below Blackstone Edge lies Soyland Moor, and the wooded valley of Cragg Vale, where the coiners lived. Turning westwards, my eyes follow the pylons along the skyline towards Stoodley Pike and its eponymous monument. A famous local landmark, the original Stoodley Pike Monument was built in 1815 to commemorate the defeat of Napoleon. It collapsed in 1854, the result of general neglect, aided and abetted by the local weather, and a well-aimed lightning strike. The monument was rebuilt in 1856 to mark the end of the Crimean War. Its 121-feet spike stands 402 metres above sea-level (1,319 feet in old money): just one metre higher than where I'm standing right now, next to this thirty-times-smaller monument. On this raised, gritstone plateau, all the local summits are roughly the same height: around 400 metres.

Continuing its westward sweep, my gaze passes across the upper Calder Valley, with Hebden Bridge hidden out-of-sight below; past another gritstone outcrop, the *bride stones* of Bridestones Moor; and on to the tower of Heptonstall Church across the Hebden Water valley. The tower is only just visible above the heather and camber of the hill on which I'm standing. Its silhouetted profile always reminds me of Batman's cowl. The American poet Sylvia Plath is buried over there, as is 'King' David Hartley, leader of the Cragg Vale coiners, hanged near York in 1770.

My gaze turns northwards, across the forested upper reaches of Hebden Dale and the Hardcastle Crags, a local beauty-spot immortalised in verse by Ms Plath. Further north still is *The Packhorse Inn*, known locally as *The Ridge*, with Widdop Reservoir and the southern flank of Pendle Hill above and behind. Then it's along the ridge concealing *Wuthering Heights* (the subject of another poem by Ms Plath), and around north to the aptly named High Brown Knoll, the local high-spot at 443 metres. The panoramic view is then cut short by a nearby heathery slope until the local wind power station flails into view. Then it's on past Halifax, the Emley Moor transmitter (the tallest freestanding structure in Great Britain), more turbines, and a distant view of the M62 motorway as it divides either side of a famously isolated farmhouse. Then, after a couple more transmitters, I'm looking back towards Blackstone Edge.

I run my fingers along the three brass grooves set into the flat top of the trig point. Radiating at 120° from each other, they were designed for mounting a theodolite. As I don't have a theodolite, I take out my flask of hot water and, using the trig point as a table, make myself a brew. Red grouse are kicking up a commotion somewhere in the heather behind me. Some sort of territorial dispute, by the sound of it. It might only be late January, but spring is already in the air.

Trig point: short for *trigonometrical point*; from the Greek *trigonon*, meaning 'triangle', and *-metron*, meaning 'measure'. Neither a monument nor a summit-marker, this squat pillar is all about measuring triangles.

Any three points which aren't in a straight line define a triangle. But you don't need to know the positions of all three of those points to determine the exact position of the triangle. For example, you might know the position of two of the triangle's corners (or *vertices*), and the direction from each of those vertices to the third vertex. From that, you can work out the position of the third vertex: there is only one possible solution. It's a pretty simple calculation, but, using the same principles, you can measure and map an entire country—or even a planet. Those principles are called *geometry*, again from the Greek: *geo*, meaning 'earth', and *-metria*, meaning 'measurement'. The geometry you studied at school might have seemed like a load of arcane nonsense about polygons, but it was really about measuring and mapping things. And by far the easiest way to map lots of things on a large, geographical scale is to use triangles.

The chap generally credited with first using triangles to measure things in this way was the sixth-century-B.C.E. philosopher Thales of Miletus. He worked out that it was possible to calculate the height of a pyramid by measuring the length of its shadow and the angle of the sun—in other words, by using triangles. Thales used similar geometrical principles to calculate the distances of ships out at sea.

Three-hundred-or-so years later, Eratosthenes of Cyrene (a Greek colony in modern-day Libya) used simple geometry to estimate the size of the earth. He had heard that, in the city of Swenet (modern-day Aswan in Egypt), the sun shone directly down a well at midday on the summer solstice. In other words, the sun was directly overhead. Farther north, where Eratosthenes lived, in Alexandria, the sun was not directly overhead. Eratosthenes calculated the angle of the sun from the vertical at noon at Alexandria on the summer solstice by measuring the shadow-length of a pillar of known height. He found it to be one-fiftieth of a complete circle (7.2° in modern parlance). Making the assumption that Alexandria was directly north of Swenet, and that the distance between the two cities, as previously measured by surveyors, was 5,000 stadia (an ancient measure of distance), Eratosthenes calculated the polar circumference of the earth to be 250,000 stadia (360° ÷ 7.2° × 5,000 stadia)—although this figure is reported as 252,000 stadia by most ancient sources, indicating that Eratosthenes made some adjustments to his calculation. Unfortunately, there were several variants of the ancient *stadion* measure, and which one Eratosthenes used is a hotly debated subject. The result he obtained for the polar circumference of the earth is generally reckoned to be around 10–30% too big, although some estimates put him within 2%. In any event, he was in the right ball park.

I remember my first lesson in practical geometry at

primary school. We used a combination of cardboard protractors, plumb-lines, and drinking straws for sights to measure the angle subtended by the top of a tree from a point a known distance away from its base. Back in the classroom, we drew *similar triangles* on paper to reflect the measurements we had taken, thereby enabling us to calculate the height of the tree. I'd never heard of Thales of Miletus, but I like to think he would have been proud of us repeating his experiment, albeit with a tree instead of a pyramid. Thirteen or so years later, for a physics dissertation at Durham University, I photographed the Moon through a telescope and calculated the depths of a number of lunar craters based on the length of their shadows. The geometry was slightly more complicated, but it still boiled down to triangles. With triangles, it turns out, you can also measure things beyond the earth. Indeed, in exactly the same way that Thales measured the distance of ships out at sea, you can even measure the distance to nearby stars using the diameter of the earth's orbit around the sun as one side of a triangle and by taking two bearings on the star six months—that is half an earth-orbit—apart.

Triangles can also help you to work out where you are. On a local level, for example, if you were here with me right now, you might take compass bearings on Blackstone Edge and the crags on Bridestones Moor to work out our position on the Ordnance Survey map. The two bearings to known fixed points would be enough to allow you to construct a unique triangle on the map. The third point of the triangle drawn on the map would indicate our position. To decrease the margin of error in your readings, you might take additional bearings on other identifiable objects in the landscape. To make extra, extra sure, or to save time, you might simply ask me: I know exactly where we are, thank you very much.

On a wider, global scale, if you know the date and time, and which way is north, you can measure the position of the sun, or other celestial bodies, to calculate your location on the surface of the earth. Working out your latitude—how far north or south you are from the equator—was always relatively simple, provided you knew the date: simply measure the angle of the noonday sun above the horizon (or at night, the angle of some reference star), then look up your latitude in the appropriate published tables. But knowing how far east or west you are—your longitude—was a much bigger problem until a couple of hundred years ago. To work out your longitude, you need to know what time it is in London, home of the Greenwich *Prime Meridian*, from which all longitudes are determined. If you know the time now at Greenwich, and you know the local time where you are—as determined from the sun at local noon, or by the rising or setting of other heavenly bodies—you can work out the time difference between where you are and Greenwich, and, hence, your longitude: every four minutes' time difference equates to one degree of longitude. But, to do this, you need to know the time now at Greenwich. This means you need an accurate clock set to Greenwich time—a clock which can also work at sea, if you're crossing oceans—and such clocks weren't invented until the second half of the eighteenth century.

Once accurate ships' chronometers became generally available, although still far from cheap, the British Admiralty dispatched a special ship whose mission, amongst other things, was to gather accurate measurements of the longitudes of key ports of call around the world. This would allow other ships visiting those ports to re-set their own chronometers to Greenwich time, based on the certain knowledge that the longitudes of those places had already been accurately established. The captain of the special survey ship, a stickler for detail, took no less than twenty-two chronometers with him on his five-year voyage: eleven supplied by the Admiralty, five on loan, and six paid for out of his own pocket. As a result of that voyage, he obtained highly accurate measurements of numerous key points on the surface of the earth—measurements which could still be relied on to this day. The perfectionist, and rather temperamental ship's captain was named Robert FitzRoy. His ship was named *H.M.S. Beagle*. His companion on the voyage was a 22-year-old gentleman who showed considerable promise as a man of science.

The technique of using triangles to work out where you are on a map can also be used in reverse to draw up the map in the first place. The technique is known as *triangulation*, and was first proposed in the mid-sixteenth century by the Flemish mathematician Gemma Frisius (Jemma the Frisian). He described his technique in a booklet entitled *Libellus de Locorum Describendum Ratione* (*Little Book Concerning a Method for Describing Places*).

It's difficult to measure accurate distances across rough terrain—or at least it was until radar, lasers, and other modern range-finding devices became available. Suppose I were trying to make a map of this area and needed to measure the distance from this trig point to the crags on Bridestones Moor. They're about four or five miles away, but there's no way I could get an accurate measurement on foot. Between here and there lie steep, winding valleys hundreds of feet deep, rivers, slippery slopes, drystone walls, bogs, tussocky heather, woods, and settlements. For much of the journey between the two points, either this trig point or the crags or both would be hidden from view, making keeping to a straight line almost impossible. And, to make an accurate map, I would have to make many hundreds of such measurements. It wouldn't be practical.

But measuring triangles is far easier and quicker. From this trig point, given the right equipment, namely a theodolite, I could easily measure the angle between the crags on Bridestones Moor and some other fixed point—the summit of Crow Hill across the valley to the south, say. I could then climb Crow Hill and measure the angle between this trig point and the crags on Bridestones Moor. That would be enough to give me the shape of the triangle made by the trig point, the crags, and Crow Hill. If I wanted to check my readings, I could go over to the crags on Bridestones Moor and measure the angle between the other two points. The three measured angles should add up to 180° (because the internal angles of *all* triangles add up to 180°). If they didn't, I would know that at least one of my measurements must be wrong, so I'd better go back and check them. Having established the shape of my triangle, I could then use each side of that triangle as the basis for establishing further triangles in the landscape. In this way, I could establish a network of triangles criss-crossing the terrain, the precise shapes of which would all have been checked for error.

But that would only give me the *shapes* of the triangles. By then, I would have an accurate map of key features in the landscape, but the map would have no scale. I still wouldn't know how far it is from here to the crags on Bridestones Moor. If I wanted an accurate *scale* map, I wouldn't be able to avoid measuring some distances. But here's where the power of the triangulation technique really kicks in: I would only ever need to measure *one* distance. Once I'd established the length of a single side of *any one* of my triangles, I would know the scale of my map, so the lengths of the sides of all of the other triangles would be trivial to calculate. So, all I would need to do is find a reasonably long stretch of flat land, without any valleys or bogs, accurately measure a straight line, and incorporate that line into my map. I could then calculate all of my other distances based on the length of the measured line. For this reason, the line is known as a *baseline*.

Furthermore, what works in the horizontal will also work in the vertical. I could use the same triangulation techniques to measure relative heights. For example, I could measure the angle of elevation between this trig point and the crags on Bridestones Moor, and between here and Crow Hill, and so on. Once I knew the altitude above sea-level of any triangulation point on my map, I could calculate all of the others.

Establishing a baseline and reference height around here would be problematical. Fortunately, it's not necessary, as they've already been established elsewhere, and the whole country mapped using the triangulation technique I've just described. More than once, in fact.

The first detailed trigonometrical survey of Great Britain began in 1783. It began life as a rare exercise in international co-operation between two old enemies in an age of Enlightenment. At the time, Britain and France based their maps on different prime meridians: Britain on Greenwich, France on the Paris Royal Observatory. The difference between the two had never been accurately established, making it impossible to convert between the two standards. This was a particularly dangerous situation for mariners from the two countries, who needed to be able to trust each other's maps.

France had already been surveyed to a high degree of accuracy using the Paris-based meridian. So the French proposed that the British make an accurate map from Greenwich to the south coast of England, then readings be taken across the English Channel to enable the two maps, and therefore the meridians, to be reconciled.

With the endorsement of King George III and the Royal Society, Major-General William Roy and his team of Royal Engineers established a five-mile baseline on Hounslow Heath near London in 1784. Three years later, after a specially commissioned theodolite had been designed and built by Halifax-born Jesse Ramsden, Roy then began a survey from his baseline to Greenwich and down to the south coast. A series of co-ordinated readings across the Channel finally allowed the difference between the Paris and Greenwich meridians to be calculated as just over 2.3° of longitude (equating to a local time difference between the two capitals' royal observatories of 9 minutes and 19 seconds).

Roy died in 1790, but his work provided the basis and impetus for his long-held dream of a full nationwide survey. Work recommenced the following year on what has since become known as the *Principal Triangulation of Great Britain*. It was to drag on for another six decades. The surveyors were meticulous, taking into account factors such as air temperature, atmospheric diffraction, and the curvature of the earth. The latter meant that the 'triangles' surveyed were not, in fact, true, two-dimensional triangles, as the lines joining the vertices ran along the curved surface of the earth. This meant that their internal angles actually added up to slightly more than 180°.

While the survey of Great Britain was underway, the

British began a separate *Great Trigonometric Survey* of India. Foreigners were banned from entering Nepal and Tibet at the time, so the surveyors took the opportunity to measure the heights of several peaks in the Himalaya from within India. In the process, they identified one peak as being "most probably the highest in the world". Later named *Mount Everest* in honour of the previous Surveyor General of India, the height of the mountain was calculated to be exactly 29,000 feet. To avoid accusations of inexactitude, however, the surveyors added an extra two feet to the calculated height to make a more precise-sounding 29,002 feet. More recent measurements give Everest's height as 29,035 feet (8,850 metres), although the exact height of the world's highest mountain is still a contentious issue, with different countries' recognising different 'official' heights.

In 1935, eighty or so years after the Principal Triangulation of Great Britain had been completed, the Ordnance Survey decided to undertake a new, more accurate trigonometrical survey of the country using modern equipment. This project was appropriately named *The Retriangulation of Great Britain*. Work began in earnest in 1936, and wasn't completed until 1962. Several hundred permanent primary trig points were built in prominent locations, mainly on high hills. This enabled the survey to establish a network of large triangulations over the entire country. To allow more detailed surveying, several thousand further, secondary and tertiary trig points were also constructed—including the one I'm standing next to now, which was given the official trig point designation TP4144 (*Keelam*).

Triangles might be great for survey work, but they're not at all practical when it comes to giving co-ordinates. So the new triangulation network was used to define a user-friendly square grid covering the entire country. This grid forms the basis of the current Ordnance Survey grid reference system, which can be used to define any point in the country. The trig point I'm standing next to belongs in square *SE* of the grid. Its full grid reference is SE 01486 27835.

One problem with trying to impose a square grid on the curved surface of the earth is that the 'north-south' lines of the UK grid can't all represent true north-south lines on the ground. All lines of longitude converge at the north and south poles; square grid lines drawn on a flat map never converge. This means that, at most, *only one* of the grid lines on the Ordnance Survey maps of Great Britain can represent a true line of longitude. As the grid is an artificial construct, it was a matter of choice which grid line should reflect true north. Very sensibly, the Ordnance Survey chose the 2°W meridian to be the basis for their grid. They did this because the 2°W meridian runs the entire length of England, right down the middle of the country, top to bottom, Berwick-upon-Tweed to the Isle of Purbeck. For this reason, it's known as the *Central Meridian*. Choosing to base the grid on a line that runs down the centre of the map minimises the distortion between the artificial 'north-south' lines of the grid and the true north-south lines of longitude. The Scots might justifiably argue that 3°W would have been

a better choice for mapping the entire island of Great
Britain, but I'm with the Ordnance Survey on this one,
albeit for entirely parochial reasons: the 2°W meridian
runs less than 200 metres west of my house. If you want
to find True North, look for the Hebden Bridge
meridian on the map.

I take out my binoculars and train them on the crags on
Bridestones Moor. On top of the crags, silhouetted
against the skyline, I can just make out a small blip:
another trig point, TP1623. There's another, farther to
the right, past Widdop and along the ridge, TP1541, on
top of Boulsworth Hill. Turning further north, even with
the unaided eye, I can easily spot the trig point on top of
High Brown Knoll, TP3775, my trig point's nearest
sibling. To the south, needing my binoculars once more,
I can see a fourth distant trig point, TP2626, on top of
Crow Hill. There's no concrete trig point on Stoodley
Pike: the monument itself fulfils the role. I look for the
trig point on top of Blackstone Edge, but the light isn't
right today, so I can't make it out amongst the crags. I
reckon I should be able to see other trig points from
here—at Manshead End on Soyland Moor, and on
Heptonstall Moor, and elsewhere—but either I'm
looking in the wrong places, the viewing conditions
aren't right, or the trig points are hidden by features in
the terrain.

If you stand at a trig point, you should always be able
to see at least two others, weather permitting. Well,
that's not entirely true: I can think of one trig point near

here which has had an entire wood grow up around it since it was built! But it's fun to stand at a trig point, try to work out suitable locations for other trig points, and then look to see if you can spot them. Yes, I know, I really should stay in more.

Sadly, the vast majority of the trig points erected during the Retriangulation of Great Britain are now obsolete in this age of Global Positioning System satellites. A few of them still serve as calibration points or additional transmitters for the GPS, but most, like TP4144, are now mere curiosities, looked upon fondly by passing walkers.

I take out my phone, turn on its GPS app, and set it down next to my flask on top of the trig point. After a few seconds, it has picked up signals from several satellites. As when taking bearings with a compass, or with FitzRoy and his twenty-two ship's chronometers, the greater the number of independent readings, the smaller the margin of error. I read my co-ordinates from the phone, correct to within a couple of metres:

53° 44' 49" N
1° 58' 44" W

It's incredible what we take for granted these days. My phone can tell me precisely where I am. Yet the principles behind determining one's location using the GPS are fundamentally the same as the humble magnetic compass. Like the compass, the GPS allows you—or, rather, your GPS device—to triangulate your current position by taking bearings on known locations. This time, however, the triangulation points are orbiting 12,600 miles above the earth, beaming down their co-ordinates from space.

Grouse

Ten metres beyond the trig point, something explodes out of the heather. Two somethings. Twin whirlwinds of feathers and clucks heave upwards. The size of small chickens, they rise to head-height, whir in front of me, and shoot off across the heather, staccato-clucking all the way: a brace of red grouse.

I'm startled out of my wits. Grouse do this to me all the time, the bastards. I don't deal with sudden, unexpected occurrences at all well. Dog barks, car horns, things falling over, people suddenly speaking, walking into an empty room and finding someone in there: all of these things, and many more besides, are pretty much guaranteed to make me jump out of my skin. I've even been startled by my own reflection on more than one occasion. Sneaky things, mirrors. On the whole, I'm a reasonably placid person who doesn't get easily ruffled, but, for some inexplicable reason, I'm ridiculously highly strung when it comes to being taken by surprise. People find it either hysterically funny, or extremely irritating. It annoys the hell out of me. My dramatic over-reaction usually, as on this occasion, involves a reflex bellow:

HUU-UUU-UUU-URRR-RRR!

Despite having had red grouse leap out at me on more occasions than I care to mention, I've never been able to recover quickly enough from the adrenaline jolt to take a half-decent photo. By the time I've regained control of my nervous system, the birds are disappearing over the heather-line, their arched wings alternating between rapid beats and short glides. *Guk———————— guk———————— guk———————— guk———— guk———— guk——— guk— guk!* they laugh. It's a good job I've no desire to roam the Moor with a shotgun, hunting these creatures: I'd be a positive danger to anyone in the vicinity, including myself—although almost certainly not the grouse.

Our northern moorlands are Red Grouse Central. It's on account of the heather. Grouse live on heather, and are reluctant in the extreme to leave the moors. They've been spotted migrating out at sea, but such sightings are rare in the extreme. I've never even seen a grouse in the fields adjacent to the Moor. If there's no heather, they're simply not interested. Not only is heather pretty much their sole source of food, it's also their best cover: the grouse's red-brown colour provides almost perfect camouflage in the heather undergrowth. Indeed, so effective is the grouse's camouflage that it receives an honourable mention in Charles Darwin's *On the Origin of Species*:

> *When we see leaf-eating insects green, and bark-feeders mottled-grey; the alpine ptarmigan white in winter, the red-grouse the colour of heather, and the black-grouse that of peaty earth, we must believe that these tints are of service to these birds and insects in preserving them from danger. Grouse, if not destroyed at some period of their lives, would increase in countless numbers; they are known to suffer largely from birds of prey; and hawks are guided by eyesight to their prey, so much so, that on parts of the Continent persons are warned not to keep white pigeons, as being the most liable to destruction. Hence I can see no reason to doubt that natural selection might be most effective in giving the proper colour to each kind of grouse, and in keeping that colour, when once acquired, true and constant.*

Darwinian Natural Selection is alive and kicking on the Moor—as it is everywhere there's life.

The red grouse's excellent camouflage means that, unless you surprise them, as I just did, you usually hear them long before you see them—if, indeed, you get to see them at all. Throughout the year, but particularly in the breeding season, their clucks emanate from all over the Moor. They have a number of calls, the most famous being their persistent and rapid warning: *go-back! go-back! go-back!* Then there's the slow clucking noise which rapidly increases in frequency until it's almost a single note. This always reminds me of a ping-pong ball being dropped on to a table, with the intervals between successive bounces decreasing with their heights. The grouse's other call is like the bouncing-ping-pong-ball call in reverse, the interval between successive clucks getting longer and longer. This always reminds me of the noise made by those devices you see on TV game shows, where the contestant spins a large wheel which ratchet-clicks through various potential outcomes. As the wheel slows, each click takes longer than the one before, and you're never entirely sure which click will be the last. Well, substitute *clucks* for *clicks*, and that's exactly what a red grouse sounds like. Trust me on this.

Once you've heard one or other of the grouse's calls from the heather, you might look for the birds, but you'll seldom spot them. As you draw nearer, however, they will surely spot you. Then it's a matter of how much faith the individual birds place in their camouflage. Some will sit it out, trusting to their invisibility, and you'll know nothing about it. Others will eventually lose their nerve, bursting from the heather in twos and threes, sometimes silently, but more often in a chaos of clucks. If the commotion has anything like the same effect on would-be predators as it has on me, it will doubtless buy the grouse a vital couple of seconds' escape time.

They take off vertically. Grouse are stocky birds to do this, but they have no choice: the heather precludes a running take-off. Lift is determined by wing surface area to weight ratios. Larger birds are relatively heavier, requiring disproportionately larger wings. As always with Natural Selection, there are trade-offs. The grouse's vertical take-off is neither fast nor pretty, but it gets the job done. They only need to rise a metre or so above the heather, after which, they can adopt a more efficient, horizontal flight-path.

Grouse seldom seem to fly directly away from you, preferring to sweep around and away in a long curve before disappearing behind some undulation in the terrain. I suppose this curving flight allows them to keep an eye on you, rather than turning their backs. It also means their camouflaged upper feathers are angled towards you, making the moving grouse harder to track against the heather.

In flight, red grouse are no longer just reddish brown. There's a considerable amount of white on the undersides of their wings. Their feet are also covered in white feathers. The upper edges of their tails and wings can appear almost grey. Both in flight and on the ground, the birds can look decidedly pear-shaped. This shape, plus the distinctive thick, white circles around their eyes, and, in the males, their huge, inflated red eyebrows, or *wattles*, can give the grouse an almost *clown-like* appearance.

It was the grouse's comical eyebrows that endeared the birds to Sylvia Plath, long before she ever saw one. As a young girl in Massachusetts, Sylvia once found herself sitting next to a man on a bus, who entertained her with tales of the *heather-bird* and its remarkable eyebrows. She was captivated. The story of the legendary heather-bird became a treasured memory. By the time she had married local fellow poet Ted Hughes and visited these moors, Sylvia had put two and two together, and realised that the *heather-bird* was none other than the red grouse, or one of its almost indistinguishable near relatives. One day, while walking with Sylvia across the moors to the ruined farmhouse that's said to have inspired *Wuthering Heights*, Ted came across a badly injured grouse, so he captured and humanely killed it. Sylvia went ballistic: her husband of only a few weeks had killed the mythical heather-bird! Ted was stunned by Sylvia's reaction, and determined never again to kill another bird or animal. True to his resolve, he gave up shooting, but continued to fish—although he did eventually lapse back into shooting many years later, long after Sylvia was beyond caring.

Describing the grouse's feathers as *reddish brown* does them no justice. Up close, their plumage is a delightfully complex mottled pattern, giving an almost marbled effect, like the cover of an expensive Florentine notebook. The individual feathers, which I frequently come across on the Moor, are delicate scoops of softness, downy white at the quill end, brown flecked with orange and white at the other. Discarded pencil-shavings, they remind me of. Glowing embers.

The feathers on the grouse's feet are an adaptation against the cold. Most birds' feet are bare. Most birds don't have to scrat around for food in the middle of the moors in the depths of winter. It was their white, feathery feet that earned the red grouse their official scientific name: *Lagopus lagopus*. It's a concatenation of the Greek words *lagos*, meaning *hare*, and *pous* meaning *foot*. The birds' feet evidently reminded Linnaeus of the furry feet of mountain hares.

The derivation of the English word *grouse*, on the other hand, is far from clear. In his *Topographia Hibernica* (*The Topography of Ireland*), the twelfth-century traveller and clergyman Gerald of Wales refers to:

gallinae campestres, quas vulgariter grutas vocant
[the fowl of the plains, which are commonly called grutas]

So, the word *grouse* is thought possibly to have derived from the medieval Latin *grutas*, which itself might have derived from the classical Latin *grus*, meaning *crane* (the bird, not the lifting machine). But others have suggested that the word *grouse* might derive from medieval French words meaning *speckled* and *grey*, originally, perhaps, referring to the grey partridge. Let's face it, nobody has a blind clue where the word comes from. (The verb *to grouse*, meaning to grumble or complain, has nothing to do with the birds, incidentally; it seems to share the same root, or possibly derive from, the verb *to grouch*. It's a shame the two different meanings of the word *grouse* aren't connected etymologically, as the male birds' clown-like eyebrows always remind me of Groucho Marx.)

Other names, not much used nowadays, for the red grouse include the moor-cock (for males), and the moorhen (for females). The latter shouldn't be confused with the water-loving moorhen, *Gallinula chloropus*, commonly seen swimming in village ponds. More modern alternative names for the red grouse are the willow ptarmigan and the willow grouse. These monikers are, to me at least, something of a sore point:

The red grouse was once believed to be Britain's only endemic bird—that is, the only species found in Britain and nowhere else. While it was recognised that the red grouse was closely related to the willow grouse found in Scandinavia and other places surrounding the Arctic Circle, many experts thought the two species were sufficiently different to be, well, just that: *two different species*. Once again, Charles Darwin takes up the story in *On the Origin of Species*:

> *Several most experienced ornithologists consider our British red grouse as only a strongly-marked race of a Norwegian species, whereas the greater number rank it as an undoubted species peculiar to Great Britain. A wide distance between the homes of two doubtful forms leads many naturalists to rank both as distinct species; but what distance, it has been well asked, will suffice? if that between America and Europe is ample, will that between the Continent and the Azores, or Madeira, or the Canaries, or Ireland, be sufficient? It must be admitted that many forms, considered by highly-competent judges as varieties, have so perfectly the character of species that they are ranked by other highly-competent judges as good and true species. But to discuss whether they are rightly called species or varieties, before any definition of these terms has been generally accepted, is vainly to beat the air.*

Darwin was right: people have struggled for centuries to agree what we mean when we say that individual organisms are members of the same, or different, *species*. His great book was entitled *On the Origin of Species*, not *On the Definition of Species*. The closest we have to *On the Definition of Species* is the book *Defining Species* by my online mate, the Australian historian and philosopher of science John S. Wilkins. (Yes, there really is an Australian philosopher whose name isn't Bruce.) In his book, Wilkins identifies 26 different definitions of the word 'species' which have been used by scientists and philosophers over the millennia. Since writing his book, Wilkins has increased this count to 27. But, when he grouped these definitions, Wilkins concluded that they fell into seven broad camps. Or possibly just two, if he grouped them a different way. Or possibly just one. Or, if you happen to be one of those people who claim that the very idea of discrete species is meaningless, the number of valid definitions of the concept must, by definition, be zero! Species definitions are almost as difficult to count as species themselves, it would seem— although, for what it's worth, Wilkins later plumped for there being seven clearly distinct definitions of the word 'species', comprising 27 variations and mixtures.

Personally, my favourite definition of what constitutes a species is the last one in Wilkins' book, the so-called *cynical species concept*:

Taxonomic species
Species considered by a taxonomist to be members of a kind on the evidence or on the assumption they are as alike as their

offspring of hereditary relatives within a few generations. Whatever a competent taxonomist chooses to call a species.

In other words, a species is what an expert on classifying species says is a species. Deferring to authority: I can handle that. Charles Darwin, himself something of an expert on species, concluded:

> *Hereafter we shall be compelled to acknowledge that the only distinction between species and well-marked varieties is, that the latter are known, or believed, to be connected at the present day by intermediate gradations, whereas species were formerly thus connected. Hence, without quite rejecting the consideration of the present existence of intermediate gradations between any two forms, we shall be led to weigh more carefully and to value higher the actual amount of difference between them. It is quite possible that forms now generally acknowledged to be merely varieties may hereafter be thought worthy of specific names, as with the primrose and cowslip; and in this case scientific and common language will come into accordance. In short, we shall have to treat species in the same manner as those naturalists treat genera, who admit that genera are merely artificial combinations made for convenience. This may not be a cheering prospect; but we shall at least be freed from the vain search for the undiscovered and undiscoverable essence of the term species.*

Ironically, perhaps, species taxonomists themselves fall into two broad, time-honoured camps: the *lumpers* and the *splitters*. Lumpers tend to recognise fewer discrete species: they lump them together. Splitters tend to recognise more separate species: they split them apart. Darwin was something of a splitter, which is hardly surprising for someone who sought to explain how new species evolve from parent stock. His great friend and confidant the botanist Joseph Dalton Hooker was an unashamed lumper. Their different outlooks became something of a running joke between the two men.

Unfortunately, leaving the classification of the red grouse to taxonomists—today's *highly-competent judges*— has resulted in victory, for the time being at least, for the lumpers. The red grouse is now recognised to be merely a local variety of the willow grouse. Its former title as Britain's only endemic bird species was vacated, only to be claimed in August 2006 by the newly identified Scottish crossbill.

Bollocks to that, I say! I'm no taxonomist, but one thing I do know is that the real willow grouse turns pure white in winter; the red grouse doesn't. And, as red grouse almost never migrate, the two varieties are unlikely to meet. So it's plain crazy to say the red grouse is the same species as the willow grouse. Or so it seems to me. When it comes to grouse taxonomy, lump me in with Darwin and the splitters!

To his partridge-shooting friends, Charles Darwin must have seemed a splitter in another sense. In his youth, he couldn't bag enough of the things. "You care for nothing but shooting, dogs, and rat-catching, and you will be a disgrace to yourself and all your family," admonished his father. Dr Darwin was right, about the shooting at least. As Charles explained many years later in his autobiography:

In the latter part of my school life I became passionately fond of shooting; I do not believe that any one could have shown more zeal for the most holy cause than I did for shooting birds. […] When at Cambridge I used to practise throwing up my gun to my shoulder before a looking-glass to see that I threw it up straight. Another and better plan was to get a friend to wave about a lighted candle, and then to fire at it with a cap on the nipple, and if the aim was accurate the little puff of air would blow out the candle.

But, during the *Beagle* voyage, something changed:

Looking backwards, I can now perceive how my love for science gradually preponderated over every other taste. During the first two years my old passion for shooting survived in nearly full force, and I shot myself all the birds and animals for my collection; but gradually I gave up my gun more and more, and finally altogether, to my servant, as shooting interfered with my work, more especially with making out the geological structure of a country. I discovered, though unconsciously and insensibly, that the pleasure of observing and reasoning was a much higher one than that of skill and sport. That my mind became developed through my pursuits during the voyage is rendered probable by a remark made by my father, who was the most acute observer whom I ever saw, of a sceptical disposition, and far from being a believer in phrenology; for on first seeing me after the voyage, he turned round to my sisters, and exclaimed, "Why, the shape of his head is quite altered."

The game-shooting fraternity's loss was science's gain. The former potential disgrace to his family had matured during the *Beagle* voyage. Charles Darwin had become a man of science.

Darwin lost his passion for bagging game before grouse-shooting took off in a big way. Partridges and pheasants were available for shooting in estates all over Britain, but you could only shoot grouse in decent numbers on the desolate mountains and moors. These remained effectively inaccessible in the wuthering north until the advent of the railways. When the railways arrived, grouse-shooting suddenly became very big business indeed. At long last, southern toffs were able to travel up north in relative comfort to lay waste to the local fauna. Useless northern moorland estates suddenly became valuable property. Everyone who was anyone took to blasting *Lagopus lagopus* from the skies. Queen Victoria made it trendy; new breech-loading shotguns upped the brace-count. Records were broken and broken again. In 1888, Lord Walsingham, spurred on, it's thought, by the Prince of Wales having declined an invitation to his shoot, single-handedly downed 1,070 grouse in 12½ hours. That's over one per minute.

The Glorious Twelfth, they call the start of the grouse-shooting season. The Twelfth of August that is: a date written into the statute books under the *Game Act* of 1831. Most other hunting seasons start on the first day of the month in question. The grouse-shooting season used to be no exception, starting on the 1st August. But then, in 1752, Britain finally abandoned Julius Caesar's Julian Calendar and, like most of Europe before it, adopted Pope Gregory XIII's more useful Gregorian Calendar. This was by no means the last time Britain would be slow on the uptake of a sensible pan-European initiative. The calendar synchronisation required the skipping of eleven days: Wednesday, 2nd September 1752 was followed by Thursday, 14th September. Instead of sticking with the now seasonally earlier 1st August, the start of the following year's grouse-shooting season was also slipped by eleven days to prevent it from being drawn too close to the nesting season. The official end of the grouse-shooting season became 10th December (that is, the last day of November plus eleven days)—although it's usually all over bar the shouting by the end of September. It only takes a few weeks' profitable slaughter to deplete the moors of grouse for another year.

Do I sound as if I'm against grouse-shooting? There are arguments to be made both for and against, and I remained neutral for many years. Some claim, in its favour, that shooting means the moors are managed as a serious going-concern. Heather is burnt to promote new growth, bogs are drained, predators are controlled. Such moorland management undoubtedly has knock-on benefits for other species: what's good for red grouse tends to be good for other ground-nesting birds. But burning heather can damage underlying peat, as can draining bogs—which can also cause flooding and water-quality issues in the valleys below. And *predator-control* is simply a euphemism for killing animals higher up the food-chain, both legally and illegally. In particular, the illegal killing of birds of prey is a practice which greatly benefits the grouse-shooting industry, even though such killings are officially condemned by that industry as the work of a few rogue individuals. Be that as it may, in all my years walking on the Moor, I have encountered only a handful of peregrines, merlins, hobbies, and buzzards; a solitary hen harrier; and not a single red kite. Besides, even if the red grouse's predators weren't being persecuted, there would still be the issue of blasting away defenceless wild birds with shotguns for fun. I don't get the mentality. So, yes, chalk me up as against grouse-shooting.

Irrespective of the pros and cons, I'm pleased to report that grouse-shooting's popularity has dwindled considerably since it heyday. The decline seems to have begun during the Great War. Able-bodied estate managers, gamekeepers and grouse-beaters went off to Flanders for king and country, leaving few behind to support the shoots. Many of the upper-class grouse-shooters also crossed the channel to do their duty, with the aim of bagging far bigger game. Those left behind did their best, but couldn't wreak nearly as much havoc on the grouse. Ironically, the senseless carnage on the continent curtailed the annual bloodbath on the moors. The Great War was a good time for grouse.

Not that grouse numbers were determined solely, or even primarily, by how many were shot. Even before the start of the Great War, it had become apparent that, no matter how well the moors and grouse-shoots were managed, grouse populations could suddenly plummet for no apparent reason. They would rise again a few years later, in a *boom and crash* cycle. Such cycles occur elsewhere in nature, especially where there's a close-knit predator-prey relationship. The classic example is that of the Canadian lynx and its main source of food, the snowshoe hare (another *lagos* with a furry *pous*). Both lynx and hare were trapped for their fur, so scientists were able to use historical Hudson Bay Company trading records to estimate the populations of the two species retrospectively over many decades. When the estimated populations were plotted on a graph, they were seen to fluctuate spectacularly in a roughly ten-year cycle. The lynx population's fluctuations tended to lag a short way behind those of the hare, so that the two curves on the graph were slightly out of phase. The elegant, although, it turned out, over-simplistic explanation for this phenomenon was that, when hares have a successful breeding season, there are more of them around for the lynx to eat in subsequent years, so the lynx population also starts to increase. But, after a few years, there become so many lynx that the hare population goes into decline. The reduced number of hares means that there are no longer enough of them to support the increased lynx population, so the lynx numbers also begin to fall. After a while, the lynx population is sufficiently depleted that the hare numbers begin to recover. And so on.

As ever, the natural world ultimately proved more complex than the simple textbook model. It turns out that, while lynx populations do indeed seem to be determined primarily by the numbers of hares available for eating, hare populations are determined not just by lynx numbers, but by those of other predators, and by the availability of the hares' own food sources. But let's not get bogged down in details: the oscillating relationship between the Canadian lynx and the snowshoe hare is still a damn nifty observation. This cycling interdependency between predator and prey populations has also been witnessed in other pairs of species, such as ladybirds and aphids. But such neat, regular fluctuations only seem to occur when the predator species in question feeds primarily on a single prey species, and where that prey species is predated mainly by that predator. Throw a few more predator and prey species into the mix, and the species fluctuation graphs suddenly become much more chaotic.

In the early days of the twentieth century, occasional plummets in grouse numbers were attributed to 'grouse disease'—a catch-all term used to label a biological phenomenon whose cause nobody understood. Nowadays, they would no doubt call it *grouse collapse syndrome*. Eventually, grouse disease became such a financially significant problem that, in 1904, a ministerial committee was set up to determine its cause, and advise on how it might be controlled. The committee was chaired by Lord Lovat, who, as a grouse moor owner, had a vested interest in the enquiry's success. There were a number of other distinguished gentlemen on the committee, but most of the hard graft seems to have been carried out by the naturalist, medic, self-taught artist, and explorer Edward A. Wilson.

Wilson was a fascinating, highly driven young man.

His diverse skills had earned him a place on the 1901–
04 British National Antarctic Expedition. During this
expedition, Wilson and his companions, the legendary
Robert Falcon Scott and Ernest Shackleton, travelled
farther south than any previous human beings. Theirs,
incidentally, was the first British expedition to
Antarctica since James Clark Ross's expedition sixty
years earlier, the youngest member of which had been
Charles Darwin's future closest friend and incorrigible
lumper, Joseph Dalton Hooker.

Having returned to Britain from Antarctica, Wilson
threw himself into the grouse committee work. As the
official *Field Observer*, he travelled extensively throughout
the grouse moors of England and Scotland, dissecting
almost 2,000 birds at his home, and in hotel rooms,
producing marvellous watercolour illustrations, and
compiling painstaking notes. But Wilson was studying
healthy birds, so the root cause of *grouse disease* remained
a mystery. Finally, there was an outbreak of the disease,
and Wilson was able to confirm his suspicion that it was
caused by a minuscule, parasitic nematode worm,
Trichostrongylus pergracilis, which fed on the internal
organs of the adult grouse. The grouse ingested the
worms by eating young heather shoots on to which the
worms had climbed, having been excreted by their
previous hosts.

Parasites which kill their hosts are effectively
predators. The worms and grouse are, therefore, in a
closely linked predator-prey relationship, much like that
of the Canadian lynx and snowshoe hare. As in the case

of the lynx and hare, the worm and grouse are locked in a cyclical dance, resulting in booms and crashes in their populations. One way to help mitigate against grouse population crashes is to control the worms. To this end, grouse-moor managers leave piles of specially medicated grit scattered around for the grouse to ingest. I often find handfuls of the white grit on the Moor. They had me baffled for years. I'm embarrassed to say, I once thought they might be temporary way-markers for fell-runners, or even people's scattered ashes! Another way to control parasite numbers is to ensure that grouse numbers don't get too high. This logic has been seized upon by proponents of blood-sports as justification for controlled grouse-shooting—although another way to control grouse numbers would be to ensure that their natural predators, such as raptors, weasels and foxes, are allowed to do their jobs in the ecosystem, rather than being persecuted out of it. The introduction of additional predators into the mix would almost certainly destroy the boom-crash cycle. Getting rid of the gamekeepers might, counter-intuitively, be good for the game.

Sadly, Edward Wilson was never to see the final report of the committee for which he had worked so tirelessly. He dispatched his final contributions to the report from South Africa en route, once again, with Scott, to Antarctica. During this second expedition, Wilson and two colleagues made a treacherous mid-winter journey through the Antarctic night to retrieve emperor penguin eggs from one of their remote *rookeries*.

Wilson had himself recommended such an undertaking in the final report of the previous expedition. Penguins were believed to be amongst the most primitive of birds, so it was thought that a detailed study of their embryos might provide important evidence regarding the evolutionary links between birds and dinosaurs. It took Wilson and his companions over a month to travel 60 miles to the Cape Crozier penguin colony and to return to base camp with just three eggs. Their heroic journey was later documented by one of Wilson's companions, Apsley Cherry-Garrard, in his classic book about Scott's second Antarctic expedition, *The Worst Journey in the World*.

Ultimately, the penguin eggs were to prove of little scientific value, but Wilson was to be spared this disappointment. He was one of the four men who went on to accompany Scott to the South Pole, only to discover that they had been beaten there a matter of weeks earlier by the Norwegian explorer Roald Amundsen. All five men were to perish on the return trip. Wilson was there at the end, dying in the expedition's tent alongside Scott and their sole remaining companion, Henry Bowers, on or shortly after 29th March 1912. When their bodies were eventually recovered, Scott's was found to have its arm draped over his dear 'Uncle Bill': the team's affectionate nickname for Wilson.

But Wilson's untimely death might have had an important ecological legacy. In his tent, the dying Robert Scott wrote a last letter to his wife, in which he gave instructions regarding the upbringing of their only child: "make the boy interested in natural history if you can; it is better than games". It has been suggested that Scott's plans for his son's future were influenced by his great admiration for the amiable Edward Wilson. His instructions were followed, and his son, Peter Scott, grew up to become one of Britain's most famous early conservationists, as well as a talented wildlife artist. Peter Scott was one of the founders of the World Wildlife Fund (since renamed the Worldwide Fund for Nature). He even designed their iconic panda logo.

And then a third explosion: *HUU-UUU-UUU-URRR-RRR! Guk——— guk——— guk——— guk——— guk——— guk—— guk— guk!*

Stupid! Bloody! Grouse! I'll *never* get used to this! Another missed photo opportunity!

Flora

A perfect August afternoon. Blue sky, fluffy clouds, dozing sheep, cavorting rooks. A few too many heather flies for my liking, but let's not spoil the moment: it is, without doubt, *a glorious day*.

The Moor smells different today: a lazy, baking, summer smell. Honey and haymaking. Not a hint of dampness or decay. It's how summers are supposed to smell; how they used to smell, a generation ago.

Out of the breeze, the Moor sounds different too: muffled somehow, merged and indistinct. Higher ground temperatures refract sound waves skywards. Noises travel faster, but with reduced fidelity. Information is lost. A sonic heat haze.

The heather is in its prime, purple and flamboyant. I select an inviting patch on a path-side bank and sit, making the most of the dry ground. The springy heather envelops and accommodates, supporting me from all sides. It's surprisingly comfortable. No wonder they used to make beds out of the stuff.

Down at grouse-level, the heather is no longer a homogeneous mass. A twisting network of woody tunnels runs between the individual plants. Tendrils creep, grasses tussock, rushes protrude. How many creatures live down here unnoticed? Hares, rabbits, mice, beetles, snipe—perhaps even reptiles. I thought I saw a lizard once, up near the trig point. I certainly saw something, but it was out of the corner of my eye, and gone in a flash. A weasel, perhaps. But, at least I stand a chance of identifying the local fauna, when I get a decent look at it; how on Earth does anyone get to recognise all this flora?

A mass of tiny, yellow flowers peeks out at me from amongst the tussocks. I've seen these flowers up here before, of course, mostly on the drier banks. I've tried looking them up in flower-identification guides, but it turns out there are an awful lot of yellow flowers. Perhaps, if I'd studied my flower guides as closely as I studied my bird guides when I was a boy, I might have a better idea how to go about looking up plants. But where do you start? I don't claim to be any sort of bird expert, but I do at least know what kind of features to look out for when struggling to identify some unknown species: general shape, size, habitat, behaviour. This is usually enough to get me to the right section in the bird guide at least. Then there are birds' calls: I'm not particularly good at recognising those, but I know the common ones, and can compare unknown bird-calls with recordings on my phone app, and on the internet. One thing that bird-identification certainly has in its favour is that, extreme rarities aside, the number of British bird species is manageable—a couple of hundred, tops—so anyone sufficiently interested has a reasonably good chance of learning to identify a fair proportion of them.

My partner, Jen, is getting much better at identifying the birds in our garden. Before she met me, being a country girl, she had no idea how vitally important it is to be able to distinguish a dunnock from a house sparrow, or a boy chaffinch from a girl chaffinch. I still pull her leg about it at times, claiming that, before she knew me, all birds to her were either 'smaller than a crow', 'a crow', or 'bigger than a crow'. In response, Jen then usually points out how hopelessly inept I am at identifying makes and models of cars—even though, unlike with birds, their names are written on the back. She'll then, almost inevitably, remind me of the time we played *Name That Car* as we were driving down the M6 one day:

—So what's that car up ahead, Richard—the one overtaking the lorry?
—Erm... Volkswagen Polo?
—Don't be silly!
—A Fiesta, then... *I don't know!*
—You do know.
—No, I don't.
—No, you really *do* know!
—Give us a clue...
—A clue? Let's see... OK, how about this? *You're*

driving one.

I am, I admit, totally hopeless at identifying cars. I'm not much better at plants. I know some of the commoner flowers—mainly the ones Mum taught me when I was a child: bird's-foot-trefoil, bladder campion, bluebell, buttercup, clover, cow parsley, cranesbill, daisy, dandelion, dog rose, forget-me-not, foxglove, harebell (my favourite!), honeysuckle, lady's smock, meadowsweet, primrose, red campion, red dead-nettle, rosebay willowherb, sea pink, snowdrop, tufted vetch, white campion, wild garlic, and a few others. Actually, now I write it down, that's not such a bad list. But, after that, I'm pretty much clutching at bedstraws. It's not as if I'm not interested. I would dearly love to be able to tell a dandelion from a cat's-ear, and fool's parsley from genius's parsley. But I never got into plants in the same way that I got into animals, so I don't have the necessary basic skills.

Take those pointy stalks with the blobs in the middle over there, for example. They're all over the Moor, so I've tried to look them up. But where to start? Are they grass, or are they reeds, or are they sedges, or are they rushes? Or are grass, reeds, sedges and rushes different names for the same type of thing? I didn't know. I still don't know. But I eventually managed to track down the blobby stalks in a book, concluding they must be soft rushes—although, to be honest, they could just as easily be common rushes. Soft and common rushes are pretty similar, save for their subtly different seed-heads and stem cross-sections—or so my book said. Perhaps we get both types of rushes on the Moor, and I've never noticed the difference. In fact, I'd put good money on it.

The problem with plants is there are so damn many of them. Biodiversity is all well and good, but it's a pain in the arse when it comes to tracking stuff down. I've tried online *plant keys* to identify unknown flora. These ask you a series of questions to give you a whittled-down list of candidate species. But, they only really work if you understand the questions, and paid sufficient attention to the plant when you were looking at it. "What sort of flower or other kind of reproductive structure does the plant have?" asks one such program. It's a perfectly reasonable question, but the choices of answer on offer are:

- I do not know
- actinomorphic
- catkin
- compound
- cone
- slightly zygomorphic
- solitary and without perianth
- sori
- spikelet
- zygomorphic

To be fair to the excellent, extremely useful website, it does attempt to provide explanations for each of these technical terms, but I don't understand all of the explanations, and usually find myself plumping for the safe answer of *I do not know*. The same goes for other questions about the arrangement of the leaves on the stem, the shape of the leaves, the edges of the leaves, and the petioles (stalks) of the leaves. I never think to look at the leaves. Why would I? When I'm admiring some pretty, new flower, I just tend to notice what colour it is, and, if I'm really diligent, how many petals it has. I realise I'm missing a trick here, and have tried to be more observant, but I usually find I've missed some vital clue. Photographs can help, so I've started taking shots of new plants specifically for identification purposes— including the leaves, when I remember. But it's still hard work when you don't know what you're doing.

I fit my macro lens to my camera and take a photo of the tiny, yellow flowers for future reference:

It was Carl Linnaeus, the inventor of the binomial naming system for species (*Homo sapiens*, and all that) who came up with the first useful way of classifying and cataloguing plants. This was in the 1730s. His system was based on plants' sexual organs, primarily the numbers and arrangements of their 'male', pollen-producing stamens, and 'female' pistils. Linnaeus didn't claim that his system reflected natural groupings of plants, simply that it assisted in their identification. It proved very useful, though it was far from perfect. Its sexual nature also made it controversial, with one rival botanist, Johann Siegesbeck, describing it as "loathsome harlotry". Linnaeus got his own back by naming a genus of weeds after Siegesbeck.

Charles Darwin's paternal grandfather, the natural philosopher, physician, physiologist, inventor, and poet Erasmus Darwin, was a huge fan of Linnaeus, organising the translation of two of his botanical works into English. In the process, he seems to have coined several new English words concerning plant physiology, including bract, floret, and the anglicised forms of existing scientific words, such as anthers and stamens. He went on to write a long poem, inspired by Linnaeus, entitled The Loves of the Plants. The poem was later incorporated into a larger book, The Botanic Garden. As a fascinating early exercise in popular science writing, The Botanic Garden turned out to be an phenomenally successful book. Its success was aided, no doubt, by its risqué anthropomorphism—although, to modern ears, it sounds rather tame and, in the opinion of this signally unqualified judge of poetry, rather dreadful. Here's just a sample:

> *Queen of the marsh, imperial DROSERA treads*
> > *Rush-fringed banks, and moss-embroider'd beds;*
> *Redundant folds of glossy silk surround*
> > *Her slender waist, and trail upon the ground;*
> *Five sister-nymphs collect with graceful ease,*
> > *Or spread the floating purple to the breeze;*
> *And five fair youths with duteous love comply*
> > *With each soft mandate of her moving eye.*
> *As with sweet grace her snowy neck she bows,*
> > *A zone of diamonds trembles round her brows;*
> *Bright shines the silver halo, as she turns;*
> > *And, as she steps, the living lustre burns.*

In a footnote, Darwin *grandpère* explains the imagery:

> [Drosera:] *Sun-dew. Five males* [stamens], *five females* [pistils]. *The leaves of this marsh-plant are purple, and have a fringe very unlike other vegetable productions. And, which is curious, at the point of every thread of this erect fringe stands a pellucid drop of mucilage, resembling a ducal coronet. This mucus is a secretion from certain glands, and like the viscous material round the flower-stalks of Silene (catchfly) prevents small insects from infesting the leaves. As the ear-wax in animals seems to be in part designed to prevent fleas and other insects from getting into their ears.*

Hopeless though I am at identifying plants, I would know *imperial Drosera* the second I laid eyes on her. Indeed, I have sought her in vain on the Moor. The plant grows up here, I'm sure of it. Round-leaved sundew, *Drosera rotundifolia*—a plant which inspired at least one other Darwin to put pen to paper. Erasmus's grandson takes up the story:

> *During the summer of 1860, I was surprised by finding how large a number of insects were caught by the leaves of the common sun-dew (Drosera rotundifolia) on a heath in Sussex. I had heard that insects were thus caught, but knew nothing further on the subject. [...] Many plants cause the death of insects, for instance the sticky buds of the horse-chestnut (Aesculus hippocastanum), without thereby receiving, as far as we can perceive, any advantage; but it was soon evident that Drosera was excellently adapted for the special purpose of catching insects, so that the subject seemed well worthy of investigation.*
>
> *The results have proved highly remarkable; the more important ones being—firstly, the extraordinary sensitiveness of the glands to slight pressure and to minute doses of certain nitrogenous fluids, as shown by the movements of the so-called hairs or tentacles; secondly, the power possessed by the leaves of rendering soluble or digesting nitrogenous substances, and of afterwards absorbing them; thirdly, the changes which take place within the cells of the tentacles, when the glands are excited in various ways.*

This is so typical of Charles Darwin: a small observation seeming *worthy of investigation*, leading to speculation, experimentation, and eventual publication. The above passage is taken from the beginning of his 1875 book, *Insectivorous Plants*, published fifteen years after his chance encounter with *Drosera rotundifolia*. Later in the book, Darwin describes his experiments to gauge the plant's sensitivity to the aforementioned *nitrogenous fluids*, which included milk, albumen, infusions of raw meat, and human urine—although he tactfully fails to mention whose urine it was. Shortly after carrying out these experiments, Darwin wrote to his friend Joseph Dalton Hooker, saying:

> *Latterly I have done nothing here; but at first I amused myself with a few observations on the insect-catching power of Drosera; and I must consult you some time whether my 'twaddle' is worth communicating to the Linnean Society.*

(That would be the Linnean Society named in honour of Carl Linnaeus, incidentally.)

Darwin junior's long-suffering wife, the saintly Emma, wrote to another close family friend about her husband's *twaddlish* experiments, wryly observing:

> *At present he is treating Drosera just like a living creature, and I suppose he hopes to end in proving it to be an animal.*

Maybe not quite an animal, but Darwin did end up proving conclusively that, contrary to what his own grandfather had believed, *Drosera rotundifolia* traps insects in its sticky *coronet* not to prevent them from infesting its leaves, but in order to digest them. The plant lives in nutrient-poor soils, such as on heaths and moorland. Insects are, it turns out, a useful alternative source of nutrients. Life, as always, is good at finding new ways.

Insects! Don't get me started on insects! Insects are worse than plants. Nobody is sure of the exact numbers, but there are tens of thousands of insect species in Britain alone: 7,000 flies, 6,000 parasitic wasps, 4,000 beetles, give or take. How does even an expert stand a chance of identifying all of those, let alone some clueless idiot coming across a pretty, purple-hemmed beetle out on a moor somewhere and idly wondering what it might be?

But hope might be at hand. Being able to identify species quickly in the field—or on the Moor—would be a boon for serious scientists and other professionals, as well as clueless idiots. It's a problem crying out for a technological solution. We don't have one yet, but it's only a matter of time. DNA analysis is one obvious approach.

DNA analysis is expensive and time-consuming, but it's becoming less expensive and time-consuming every year. There is a long-term trend in information technology for computer processors to double in power, or halve in price, every eighteen months or so. This is known as *Moore's Law*, in honour of Gordon E. Moore, one of the founders of the chip manufacturer Intel, who first drew attention to the trend in 1965. It has held true ever since. DNA analysis seems to be following a similar trend—one which, if anything, is outstripping Moore's Law. If this trend continues, and there's no reason to think it won't, it surely can't be many years before we're able to pop a small sample of some unknown organism into our mobile phones, press a button, and be told exactly what species it came from. There are all sorts of applications for such technology, from crime scene investigation to preventing international trade in endangered species, and from helping ecologists to do their jobs to letting the likes of me and you identify what we've just discovered on our walk.

Such possibilities, however, raise once again the question of what we mean when we refer to 'a species'. A number of the 27 variations of species definitions identified by John S. Wilkins in his book *Defining Species* involve genetic considerations. This is hardly surprising: the closer the relationship between two organisms, the closer the similarity of their genes. The question remains, however, *how close* must two organisms' genes be before we say that they are members of the same species? My personal set of genes (my *genome*) is different from yours, but it has more in common with yours than either of our genomes has in common with the genome of, say, one of the sheep grazing over there in the heather. Furthermore, my genome and the sheep's, both being animal genomes, have more in common with each other than either of them has in common with any of the genomes of the individual heather plants amongst which the sheep is grazing. But which sections of our respective genomes would a geneticist need to look at to separate the heather from the human, and the human from the sheep?

Throughout the world, scientists now routinely extract and read DNA from specimens. This process is known as *DNA sequencing*. Computer programs can compare DNA sequences from the different specimens to establish which sections of their genomes (technical name, *loci*) might be used to identify or differentiate them. But a suitable locus for establishing the difference between samples of, say, common rushes and soft rushes won't necessarily be a suitable locus for establishing the difference between samples of red campion and white campion. To make at-scene DNA identification of species a practicality, it would be helpful if the number of loci that need to be analysed could be kept to a minimum.

Fortunately, in the same way that late-eighteenth-century cartographers realised that it was important to be able to link together geographical maps based on the rival Greenwich and Paris meridians (which eventually led to agreement, in principal, to standardise on Greenwich in 1884), geneticists have realised that they need to agree standard genetic loci to sequence to assist in species identification. A single such locus had already been agreed for all animals when the *Consortium for the Barcode of Life (CBOL) Plant Working Group* was set up to identify one or more loci to serve as standard *DNA barcodes* for identifying land plants. My friend Karen was one of the 52 geneticists and botanists who designed and carried out research for the working group. The group's findings and recommendations were published in 2009 in a paper entitled *A DNA Barcode for Land Plants*. In the end, they identified two genetic loci to be used as a standard barcode for land plants: the poetically named *rbcL* and *matK*. (No, me neither.)

It will be some years yet, I reckon, before I have a DNA barcoding app on my phone. Which doesn't exactly help in the immediate problem of identifying the pretty yellow flowers I've just photographed. Perhaps I could take a sample and post it to Karen, requesting that she carry out a DNA sequence and run the results through the *GenBank* database. But that would be the costly, time-consuming option—and I dare say Karen has more pressing matters to deal with. So perhaps I should stick with more traditional plant-identification techniques for the time being. Time to head home, get out the identification guides, call up the online plant key, and finally work out, with a reasonable degree of confidence, that the little yellow flowers I saw on the Moor were none other than *Potentilla erecta*, common tormentil.

Tea break

Time for a brew.

It was raining earlier, so a dry seat is out of the question. I make my way to the drystone wall at the edge of the Moor and lean against one of the new gates, taking in the view across the valley. The sheep in the top field size me up through gun-emplacement eyes. Having determined I'm no threat, and that I haven't brought corn, they return to the serious business of grazing. A couple of fields away, a man in a high-visibility jacket is rebuilding a wall. His female companion, dressed in an even-higher-visibility chequered lumber jacket, acts as supervisor. He's done a wonderful job so far, but has many months to go. Drystone walling is skilful, time-consuming work. It's harder than it looks. I've tried it, and I was rubbish. It's one of the many under-appreciated, dying crafts that helped shape the British countryside: walling, hedging, draining, coppicing. Few people have time for it these days. Wire fences are so much cheaper, and easier to maintain.

It's raining up the valley towards Todmorden, but I

should be all right: the northerly wind is pushing the shower southwards towards Blackstone Edge.

I take my vacuum flask out of my camera bag and place it on top of the gate. It took me ages to find the perfect flask for the Moor Walk. I have a cupboard full of imperfect ones back at home: too big, too small, too fiddly, and a couple which leak. All I ever required, it turned out, was a mug-sized flask which would fit into a pocket or camera bag; one without any stupid cups or handles; one which I could drink from directly, rather than having to faff about. As an added bonus, my flask's cap contains a secret compartment—officially, some sort of pressure-release valve—which I use to store my tea bag. It took me years to realise that the solution to horrible, stewed, vacuum-flask tea was simply to carry hot water in the flask and brew the tea from a bag at scene. I don't bother with milk either: too much hassle. And it has to be tea, not coffee. *Yorkshire Tea*™, obviously.

We brew some of the best tea here, in West Yorkshire. It's down to the water. It doesn't contain any disgusting chalk or limestone. Our water is soft, clear, and tastes, well, how water is *supposed* to taste: *tasteless*. They keep talking about linking us up to some sort of national water grid, so that all of our 'spare' water can be sent to the desiccated masses down south. Hands off! We don't want your nasty, chalky water coming anywhere near our supply, thank you very much!

I run my thumb over the two small dents on the side of the flask. Every dent has a tale. These are from the time I was sitting on my favourite rock in Anglesey before breakfast one September morning. I was looking out to sea, wondering what would come along next: *nature waiting*, as I like to think of it. As it happened, the next thing to come along was a grey seal. Its head emerged from the water without warning, just five metres in front of me. *HUU-UUU-UUU-URRR-RRR!* I bellowed, sending my brand new vacuum flask tumbling on to the rocks. The seal looked at me quizzically. Perhaps he thought I'd emitted some sort of mating call.

The vacuum flash is a wonderful British invention. It was invented in the final decade of the nineteenth century by the brilliant Scottish chemist and physicist James Dewar. At the time, Dewar's research centred on the liquefaction of gases. In 1891, he designed and built the first equipment capable of large-scale production of liquid oxygen. In 1898, he became the first person to liquefy hydrogen: a magnificent achievement. While carrying out this work, Dewar puzzled over the best way to store the liquids he was producing, and came up with the idea of the vacuum flask—or *Dewar flask*, as many chemists still call it. In fact, I think I'll make a point of calling it that from now on.

The design of the Dewar flask is elegantly simple. It's actually two flasks, one inside the other, joined at the neck. The gap between the flasks is partially evacuated of air to reduce heat transfer by conduction and convection. Silvering the sides of the flasks helps reflect back radiated heat. The open neck of the nested flasks is sealed with a heavily insulated stopper. All of which mean that any hot objects placed within a Dewar flask remain hot for longer, and any cold objects remain cold. But not forever: some heat will always pass across the gap between the flasks, and through the stopper and seal.

Sadly, having a typical Briton's entrepreneurial flair, Dewar neglected to patent his brilliant invention. It was subsequently patented and mass-produced as a consumer product by a new company whose name became synonymous with domestic Dewar flasks. Dewar sued and lost. The *Thermos*™ brand is still going strong.

I filled my Dewar flask with boiling water about an hour ago. The water will still be scalding hot inside. The flask, despite its nostalgic dents, will have contained most of the heat. Had I, instead, filled my flask with ice-cold water, however, it would be incorrect to say that the flask had *contained most of the cold*; the flask would actually have prevented heat from the air outside getting in. This might sound like splitting hairs, but it's an important distinction. It illustrates a principle—indeed, a scientific *law*—which is generally recognised to be the most important idea in all of science: the *Second Law of Thermodynamics*.

First things first: what is the *First Law of Thermodynamics*? Strange as it might seem, that would actually be *second* things first, for there is also a *Zeroth Law*. The Zeroth Law is so basic that it belongs first, but they only thought to give it a number after they had already numbered the other laws. Being pragmatic scientists, therefore, they assigned it the number zero! Putting it over-simply, the Zeroth Law states that two objects which are both the same temperature as a third object are also the same temperature as each other. This might sound patently obvious—especially the way I've expressed it—but it's the sort of thing you need to state up-front.

The First Law of Thermodynamics is effectively what we were all taught at school as the *Principle of Conservation of Energy*. Again, putting it over-simply, the First Law states that energy is never created or lost, it's only ever converted between different forms. When you lift a weight, for example, the chemical energy in your muscles is converted, by way of mechanical energy in your arm, into potential energy in the raised weight (plus heat—which is why lifting weights makes you hot, as well as tired). If you let go of the weight, the extra potential energy you stored in it by raising it in the earth's gravitational field is converted, as the weight falls, into kinetic energy—energy associated with moving objects. This is then converted into sound, heat and other forms of energy as the weight thuds into the ground. Albert Einstein then had to go and complicate matters (no pun intended) by stating that energy can be converted into mass, and mass into energy, according to the most famous equation in all of science:

$$E = mc^2$$

In other words, counter-intuitively, mass is just another

form of energy. So, when the First Law of Thermodynamics states that energy is always conserved, it really means that *mass and energy combined* are always conserved.

Which brings us to the Second Law.

Because it has such profound implications, the Second Law of Thermodynamics can be, and has been, expressed in many different ways, depending on the particular application being discussed. In fact, the person generally credited with first expressing an early version of the Second Law, the French engineer Nicolas Léonard Sadi Carnot (1796–1832), could not have appreciated how far-reaching his findings would turn out to be. Carnot was primarily interested in steam engines. As a patriotic Frenchman, he was concerned at Britain's economic rise during the Industrial Revolution—a rise which Carnot attributed largely to Britain's expertise in steam engines. But, like living species, the steam engine had evolved slowly through a process of trial and error. Nobody really understood the underlying science. Carnot was determined to give steam engine design a scientific foothold. In 1824, he published his findings in a book entitled *Réflexions sur la Puissance Motive du Feu* (*Reflections on the Motive Power of Fire*), in which he showed that steam engines can only work when heat passes through them from a hot area (the boiler) to a cooler area (the outside world). The greater the temperature difference, the more efficient the engine. Importantly, Carnot also realised that engines couldn't work by transferring heat the other way, from the cooler outside world into the hot boiler. Tragically, Carnot was to die of cholera eight years later, his book largely ignored. More tragically, to the history of science at least, most of his notebooks were burnt after his death, due to fears that they might be contaminated with the disease that had killed him.

A generation later, Carnot's work was picked up by a number of other scientists, most notably the German mathematician and physicist Rudolf Clausius, and his British contemporary and counterpart, the Belfast-born William Thomson (later Lord Kelvin). It was Clausius who first formally re-expressed what Carnot had said in more general terms, stating that "No process is possible whose sole result is the transfer of heat from a body of lower temperature to a body of higher temperature." That is to say, heat will never spontaneously flow from a cold object to a hotter object. Which is why, if my Dewar flask were filled with cold water, the flask would keep the heat out, not the cold in.

Thompson, the man who invented the word *thermodynamics*, expressed the Second Law in a different way, stating, "No process is possible in which the sole result is the absorption of heat from a reservoir and its complete conversion into work." In other words, no engine can ever be 100% efficient. Heat—that is, energy—must always be lost somewhere in the process. And the only place it can ultimately be lost to is the outside world. The colder external atmosphere is, it turns out, every bit as important to a steam engine—or any other engine—as the source of heat.

One implication of energy's always being lost somewhere in the process is that you can't build a perpetual motion machine. They're physically impossible. Which explains why the British Patent Office automatically refuses all patent applications for such mythical devices.

Clausius and Thomson weren't just talking about steam engines; they were talking about *all* physical and chemical processes. No process can be 100% efficient. Some energy is always lost. The concentrated energy powering an engine, or stored in a flask of hot water, will spread out into the wider world, and eventually the wider universe. Clausius gave this inexorable *spreading out* of energy the name *entropy*: highly concentrated, localised energy becoming more diffuse and disorganised. On a more general level, *everything* spreads out over time: a sugar cube dropped into a cup of tea dissolves and spreads throughout the liquid; gas escapes from an unstoppered container and fills the room; lofty mountains erode and are levelled; the individual air molecules in Carnot's dying breath spread throughout the atmosphere, and you are breathing in some of them right now, there being far more air molecules in a dying man's lungs than there are lungfuls of air in the atmosphere.

In the mid-twentieth century, the concept of entropy also began to be applied, by analogy, to information. Like energy, information dissipates inexorably over time as it is misread, miscopied, or destroyed. All information is ultimately lost.

What the Second Law of Thermodynamics really says is that *things wear out*. Walls fall over, flasks get dented, notebooks are destroyed, stuff is forgotten. In the end, *everything* wears out. There's absolutely nothing any of us can do about this. While we might try to fight entropy—by replenishing the hot water in our Dewar flasks, for example, or by mending a collapsed drystone wall—we can only do so by creating more entropy elsewhere—by boiling a kettle, or by feeding the drystone waller. Overall, we always create more entropy than we get rid of. But Thompson realised that entropy can't continue increasing indefinitely. At some point in the unimaginably distant future, everything will have spread and levelled to such an extent that there will be insufficient heat differences anywhere in the universe to power any more processes. At this point, no further work will be possible. Entropy will finally have maxed-out. This tragic, unavoidable future state is known as *the Heat-Death of the Universe*. But until that fateful day, which no creature will live to see, Entropy will continue her inexorable rise.

Another way to express the Second Law of Thermodynamics, therefore, is in terms of entropy, by saying that *entropy never decreases in a closed system*. A 'closed system' is one which is totally isolated from external energy sources. While entropy might, for a while, decrease on a local scale, throughout the closed system as a whole, total entropy is always increasing. There is more entropy in the universe now than there was a second ago.

Some people whose religious views prevent them from accepting the very idea of evolution have tried to fight science with science, arguing that Darwinian evolution breaks the Second Law of Thermodynamics. What is evolution, if not the spontaneous organisation of matter—that is, a *decrease* in entropy? If evolution really did break the Second Law of Thermodynamics, it would be in a hell of a lot of trouble—in fact, we would have to reject the idea. But why stop at evolution? Isn't life itself the spontaneous organisation of matter? Every one of us was conceived as a single cell; a cell which went on to assemble a spectacularly complex body comprising tens of trillions of specialist cells. Fortunately for life on Earth, creationists who cite the Second Law of Thermodynamics as disproof of evolution conveniently overlook one rather important consideration: the earth is *not* a closed system; it has a massive external energy source—an energy source which we call *the sun*. While evolution—and life itself—does, indeed, represent a local decrease in entropy, that decrease is more than compensated for by the massive increase in entropy brought about as the sun's energy is continuously released into the solar system. Indeed, it's this release of energy that powers the evolutionary process, that powers life itself.

But the Laws of Thermodynamics did lead to one huge headache for Charles Darwin. It was William Thomson himself who gave Darwin the headache—a headache which he was never able to shake. Thompson realised that it should be possible to use the Laws of

Thermodynamics to calculate the "age of the Earth as an abode fitted for life". That is, to place an upper limit on the age of life on Earth. Thomson approached the problem from two different directions, by considering independently the ages of the sun and earth. The sun, he reasoned, must have formed from a cloud of hydrogen gas under the influence of gravity. As the atoms within the gas drew together, gravitational energy was converted into heat, and the sun began to shine. Thomson calculated that, based on current observations, the sun could have been shining—thereby being capable of supporting life on Earth—for no more than approximately 20 million years. He then went on to consider the age of the earth. The earth must once have been a molten mass, which clearly couldn't support life. As the planet cooled, radiating heat into space, a crust eventually formed. The age of the earth's crust set an independent upper limit on the age of life on Earth. Once again, Thomson performed the necessary thermodynamic calculations, and came up with an answer of 100 million years: five times greater than the limit set by his solar calculation, but within an order of magnitude. In later calculations, he revised this second figure downwards, bringing it much more in line with the first.

The results of Thomson's calculations cast doubt on Darwin's recently published theory of evolution. They simply didn't allow enough time for life on Earth to have evolved into all its different forms. Indeed, in the first edition of *On the Origin of Species*, Darwin had used estimates of geological erosion rates to calculate the age of the Weald in Southern England. He arrived at a figure of 300 million years—an figure which Thomson criticised for being far too great. But, having spent more than twenty years amassing evidence in its support, Darwin had, by now, sufficient confidence in his own theory to put on a brave face, writing to his friend Joseph Dalton Hooker:

> *I am bigoted to the last inch, and will not yield. I cannot think how you can attach so much weight to the physicists, seeing how Hopkins, Hennessey, Haughton, and Thomson have enormously disagreed about the rate of cooling of the crust;*

and to another correspondent:

> *I have that profound respect for mathematics which profound ignorance gives, but I cannot help observing that when applied to uncertain subjects, such as geology, it gives as uncertain results as geologists arrive at by other means; for instance, how Thomson and others differ about the thickness of the crust of the earth and the rate of cooling.*

Darwin knew that Thomson, undoubtedly one of the most brilliant physicists of his or any other day, must have been wrong. But he couldn't prove it. Neither could anyone else. Darwin went to his grave in Westminster Abbey with the paradox unresolved. Resolution eventually came thanks to two new discoveries. The first, the discovery of radioactivity by the French physicist Antoine Henri Becquerel in 1896, provided the earth with a previously unknown additional source of heat, which would keep the cooling planet warmer for longer. With hindsight, we now also know that Thompson failed to take into account heat convection within the earth's mantle. In reality, though, Thomson knew that his cooling-earth calculation was by far the weaker of the two: it made far more assumptions. It had only survived rigorous scientific scrutiny because it happened to give broadly the same answer as his more scientifically valid calculation of the maximum age of the sun. Thomson's age-of-the-sun calculation wasn't falsified until the 1930s, with the discovery of a second previously unknown source of energy—a source of energy which occurs with abundance in the sun— thermonuclear fusion.

I remove my tea bag from its secret compartment and unscrew the lid of my Dewar flask. Heat and water vapour rise around my fingers and spread out into the atmosphere. Time to put this concentrated source of energy to good use. Holding on to a corner, I dunk the tea bag up and down in the flask. Tea molecules spread out from the bag and into the hot water. Soon they will spread out into me—and then, who knows where? Entropy continues her inexorable rise. Fortunately, far away in some much warmer climate, a bush of the genus *Camellia* will be fighting this chaos. The product of several hundred million years of Darwinian evolution on this living planet, that bush will be doing its bit. It will be capturing energy radiated by the massive local thermonuclear-powered entropy generator that we call the sun, and using it to convert diffuse molecules taken from the air and soil into new tea leaves. Entropy always wins, but Life keeps fighting its corner.

That's what life is all about.

Heather

I touch the trig point to make it official, then follow the path north along the edge. After a couple of hundred metres, the convex curve of the hill drops away and opens out, revealing a wider view of the western end of the Moor with fields and valley beyond.

It's mid-August. The heather is in flower. The moors radiate purple as far as the eye can see.

Ted Hughes once used the word *euphoria* to describe the heather on this very moor. Poet Laureates have a way with words: *euphoria* is exactly right. His wife, Sylvia Plath, on the other hand, worried that, if she paid the roots of the Yorkshire heather too close attention, her bones might end up whitening amongst them. With such differing views on something as innocuous as heather, is it any wonder their marriage didn't run smoothly? As it happened, Sylvia needn't have worried: her bones now lie safely within Heptonstall churchyard, just across the valley.

I'm with Ted on this one. When the heather is in flower, the moors are transformed. Gone, the usual drab brown; it's purple-pink all the way to the horizon. *Heather purple*: the colour of my soul.

It's not until you see the moors in full flower that you realise just how much heather there is, and how many moors there are. Look at it all! Not just a *euphoria*, but an *extravagance*. Far too showy for Yorkshire, yet utterly Yorkshire. Utterly Derbyshire, too—and Cumbria, Wales and Scotland. Heather defines and unites the British highlands like no other plant. In mid- to late-August—a month named in honour of the first Roman emperor—highland Britain turns imperial purple.

Heather belongs to the *Ericaceae*: a family of shrubs that thrive in poor, acid soils. Cranberry, bilberry, azalea, and the evil rhododendron are also family members. In Britain, there are three main species of heather: purple or bell heather, cross-leaved heath heather, and true or common heather, also known as ling. All three species are found on the Moor, but it's ling that predominates, growing almost anywhere that isn't too boggy. Cross-leaved heath heather grows in some of the boggier patches, while bell heather prefers drier ground. The three different species have adapted to different niches. Life is good at finding new ways.

Ling is what I'm looking down on right now. The name derives from the Old Norse. It's a favourite with crossword-setters. If you ever see the word *heather* in a cryptic clue, think *ling*:

Marrying Heather after takeover (8)
[Answer: COUP-LING]

Compassionate Heather becomes inflamed (8)
[Answer: KIND-LING]

Despising a promise in the heather (8)
[Answer: L-OATH-ING]

Britain's three species of heather were once classified in the same genus, *Erica* (another favourite word with crossword-setters). But species' classifications can change as we discover more about them. The taxonomists who rule on such matters eventually concluded that ling was sufficiently different from the other two heathers to be placed in its own genus, *Calluna*. The name derives from the ancient Greek word *Kalluno*, meaning *to sweep*: a reference to one of the plant's former uses, as a broom.

As well as for sweeping floors, heather was also traditionally used as firewood, and as bedding for animals and humans. It was also sometimes used as an alternative to hops for brewing beer, and for making rope. In some parts of the country, it was even used to mend potholes in roads. Heather is tough stuff! Nowadays, it serves mainly as food for sheep and grouse, and as a seasonal source of nectar for bees, which use it to produce a dark, mineral-rich honey.

Heather supports an extensive ecosystem. Over 100 species of British moth caterpillars feed on heather, as do countless other invertebrates. These attract small birds and mammals. An alternative name for the meadow pipit—by far the most common bird on the Moor—is the *ling-bird*. Rabbits and hares also eat heather, especially in winter, when alternative food sources become scarce. Higher up the food-chain come the raptors and other predators that hunt the smaller animals, when the gamekeepers will let them.

Actually, the moths are a particularly sore point. Jen came up here on her own a few months back and spotted a female emperor moth (or should that be an *empress moth*?). It was just sitting there, in broad daylight, on the heather. I've yet to see one. To add insult to injury, Jen even took a photo with her phone's crappy camera, which turned out to be every bit as good as anything I could have taken with my fancy macro lens.

Then there are the flies. I'll never forget my first encounter with a swarm of heather flies one sunny afternoon in late summer. I couldn't begin to guess how many there were. They danced and reeled a couple of feet above the flowering heather, on the look-out for sex, their back legs hanging beneath them like undercarriages. There's definitely a yuck factor when it comes to heather flies. I feel itchy just thinking about them. But they left me well alone, being far more interested in each other than they were in me. Not that I blame them.

From my high vantage point, I continue to scan the heather. This is a good place for grouse. Although they're found all over the Moor, they seem to congregate in greater density in the large, flat expanse just below the edge. I always make a point of looking for them here. I'll usually hear their familiar *go-back! go-back!* call, and sometimes see them take flight, but it's unusual to spot a grouse on the ground: they're too well camouflaged in the heather.

The grouse are the reason the heather is here in such abundance. It's carefully managed by people with a financial interest in keeping grouse numbers high—until *the Glorious Twelfth*, at least. Heather can live for 30–40 years, but it becomes leggy and grows less vigorously after the first few. To ensure there are plenty of fresh, young shoots for the grouse to eat, the heather is managed by controlled burning, in regular rotation. It's quite an eye-opener to see a heather moor on fire, especially at night. There's something apocalyptic about watching the hills go up in flames. Occasionally, the fires get out of hand, and the local fire-brigades have to work overtime. Most unfortunate, but the accompanying sunsets have to be seen to be believed.

Heather-burning getting out of control was a subject of considerable irritation to Gilbert White. In *The Natural History of Selbourne*, he complains:

> *Though (by statute 4 and 5 W[illiam] and Mary) c. 23, "to burn on any waste, between Candlemas and Midsummer, any grig, ling, heath and furze, goss or fern, is punishable with whipping and confinement in the house of correction;" yet, in this forest, about March or April, according to the dryness of the season, such vast heath-fires are lighted up, that they often get to a masterless head, and, catching the hedges, have sometimes been communicated to the underwoods, woods, and coppices, where great damage has ensued. The plea for these burnings is, that, when the old coat of heath, &c. is consumed, young will sprout up, and afford much tender brouze for cattle; but, where there is large old furze, the fire, following the roots, consumes the very ground; so that for hundreds of acres nothing is to be seen but smother and desolation, the whole circuit round looking like the cinders of a volcano; and, the soil being quite exhausted, no traces of vegetation are to be found for years.*

Although the burning of heather releases large amounts of carbon dioxide into the atmosphere, the practice is, in theory at least, carbon-neutral: the new heather which replaces the old re-absorbs carbon dioxide from the atmosphere as it grows. This neat equation fails to take into account any carbon dioxide released due to the burning of the underlying peat. Needless to say, it also fails to take into account the damage done to the local flora and fauna.

Heather, being a plant, is made of countless organic molecules, in particular cellulose. Cellulose is a chain of simple glucose sugar molecules, chemical formula: $C_6H_{12}O_6$. As the gamekeeper's burning torch makes contact with the organic matter in the heather, its heat provides sufficient energy to break apart the bonds between the carbon, hydrogen and oxygen atoms in the cellulose. But these atoms have great affinity: they don't like being separated, and seek other atoms to bind on to. Oxygen is particularly good at this. Oxygen released from the cellulose, and free oxygen in the atmosphere, bind on to the released carbon atoms to make carbon dioxide, and on to the hydrogen atoms to make water in the form of steam. As the atoms in the new carbon dioxide and water molecules snap into place, they release energy in the form of heat. The amount of energy released is greater than the amount of energy it took to separate the cellulose molecules in the first place. This energy now becomes available to separate further cellulose molecules, and so on. The result is a chaotic, uncontrolled chain-reaction that we call *a fire*. Provided there remains a ready supply of cellulose and atmospheric oxygen, the combustion will continue indefinitely. Incombustible compounds within the heather are left behind as residue: ash. But a significant proportion of the neatly ordered, compact, solid matter of the plant is converted into chaotic, free-floating, atmospheric gas. As always, entropy is the net winner.

When the heather grows afresh, it effectively reverses the combustion process, converting atmospheric carbon dioxide and water into organic matter. But there can be no chain-reaction this time: the energy required to separate the atoms in the airborne carbon dioxide and water molecules is greater than that which will be produced when those same atoms snap into a new configuration to form the plants' organic matter. In order to power its growth, therefore, the heather needs a reliable energy source. It achieves this by absorbing energy from that greatest of all local entropy producers, the Sun. The process by which plants use solar energy to disassemble atmospheric carbon dioxide and water molecules, and convert them into organic matter is known as *photosynthesis*. During the process, oxygen is released into the atmosphere: a useless by-product to the plants, but of considerable importance to us animals.

Moors can recover remarkably quickly after a fire. I remember an accidental roadside fire on Soyland Moor, a few miles south of here. The morning after the fire, the affected section was a smouldering mass of twisted and charred heather twigs and blackened earth. Within weeks, the black had been replaced by succulent grass. You would never have guessed there had recently been a fire there. The heather, of course, took longer to return, but there was never any doubt it would. Heather is extremely resilient. This is partly due to the sheer number of seeds it produces. It has been estimated that a single, mature heather plant produces around 100,000 seeds per year. Any seeds that aren't eaten, and that are lucky enough to find themselves in a suitable hiding place, can remain viable for up to 100 years, waiting for the land-grab opportunity afforded by the next fire, or the death of an old plant.

As in the case of the small ecological niches on top of some of the local fence-posts, the Moor is a botanical battlefield. Every individual plant is competing with its neighbours for nutrients, water and light. Heather holds the upper hand; other species struggle to gain a toe-hold. The thousands of purple acres in front of me border on a monoculture. But heather's apparent dominance is misleading. Moorland, for all its rugged, natural beauty, is a profoundly man-made landscape. Man-made and sheep-made. If you leave a moor to its own devices, shrubs and trees will soon begin to establish themselves as the older heather dies. Gorse, alder, birch and rowan will appear first, then the slower-growing trees. If there are no sheep to eat them, and no fires to destroy them, the trees will grow, and eventually cast the heather into shade. Heather doesn't like shade. It will begin to struggle as moorland gradually turns to carr, scrub, then woodland. I've seen this process in action. Twice a day, my farmer friend used to bring her cows to milk down a rough track bounded on one side by a heather-dominated slope. When she gave up dairy farming to concentrate on beef, her cattle no longer trampled through the heather four times a day. Almost immediately, rowan and silver birch began to establish themselves. Give Nature another fifty years, and I confidently predict the farm track will be bounded by woodland.

It was our prehistoric ancestors who cleared these hills of trees, keeping them treeless with fire and sheep. Once the trees were gone, the water-table will have risen, encouraging sphagnum moss, which later became peat. Wooded hills became moorland. We maintain the treeless status quo. When left to her own devices, Nature reverts to her old tricks, or finds new ways.

Identity Crisis

Like Heathcliff, I came to Yorkshire from what is now Merseyside—the Wirral in my case, Liverpool in his. Like Heathcliff, I'm a tall, dark, romantic figure—on the written page, at least. Occasionally, like Heathcliff, I carry my ill-humour on to the Moor. Today, I'm vexed. No, I'm more than vexed: I'm irked. I might even be mildly incensed.

The travel section of this week's *Observer* newspaper contained a short article describing how the latest film adaptation of Emily Brontë's *Wuthering Heights* is likely to renew interest in the three sisters from Haworth. So far, so good. But the caption beneath the photograph accompanying the article read: *Brontë country in the Yorkshire Dales*.

Let me make this perfectly clear: *Brontë Country* is most definitely *not* in the Yorkshire Dales.

The article adds insult to injury by recommending staying, "for the ultimate *Wuthering Heights* experience", at a recently restored farmhouse in Langstrothdale. That would be Langstrothdale in Upper Wharfedale, in the

Yorkshire Dales—over an hour's drive from the genuine *Wuthering Heights* experience. Langstrothdale: a landscape of pure white limestone, not dark, satanic millstone grit.

I love the Yorkshire Dales, and have a soft spot in particular for Upper Wharfedale, but how in Hell's holy name did the Yorkshire Dales manage to become associated with *Wuthering Heights?* Hands off! North Yorkshire has James Herriot, Captain Cook, and Count Dracula. The Brontës are ours. They were born near Bradford. They lived in Haworth. They were from what's now known as West Yorkshire.

I wonder, did they ever walk on this particular moor—on *the* Moor—the Brontës? They must have passed below it, on their way down the turnpike from Haworth. Branwell, the troublesome Brontë brother, certainly came this way when he worked as a clerk at Sowerby Bridge and then Luddendenfoot railway stations. An incompetent book-keeper, he was eventually fired for financial irregularities. And Branwell's sister Charlotte was married (and, less than a year later, buried) in Haworth by a vicar from Hebden Bridge, the Reverend Sutcliffe Sowden, a close friend of her husband, the equally Reverend Arthur Bell Nicholls. So it seems likely Charlotte must have passed this way too, on her way to take tea with the Reverend Sowden. Probably.

Yes, the Brontës were *ours* all right.

I blame the Americans. 1939 was when the confusion

seems to have begun, in the form of William Wyler's Academy Award-winning motion picture *Wuthering Heights*: "YEARNING... incessant as the pounding sea! LOVE... stormy as the wind-swept moors! DRYSTONE WALLS... [the posters neglected to add] white and rounded as the Yorkshire Dales!"—although the supposed *on-location* filming actually took place in Derbyshire.

But it's not just the Americans. A couple of months back, sofa-ridden with a bout of *man-flu*, I was channel-hopping in a haze of *Beechams*, when I chanced upon the 1992 film adaptation, *Emily Brontë's Wuthering Heights*, starring Sinéad O'Connor (I kid you not) as the eponymous-for-legal-reasons Emily Brontë, Ralph Fiennes as Heathcliff, and a suspiciously French-sounding Juliette Binoche as both Cathy Linton and Catherine Earnshaw—they certainly got their money's worth there. Once again, lots of lovely, totally inappropriate, Yorkshire Dales limestone scenery, interspersed this time with some genuine millstone grit—albeit most of it filmed in the North York Moors, not genuine *Brontë Country* at all. The film's theme music, needless to say, was based on a traditional West Yorkshire song from Ireland.

And as for the latest big-screen version of *Wuthering Heights*—the one the *Observer* says is rekindling interest in the Brontë sisters (who, in case I neglected to mention it, hailed from just over there, across the moors, from Haworth in *West* Yorkshire)—absolutely no prizes for guessing in which limestone-bedrocked national park the movie was filmed.

The poor marketing people charged with getting more visitors to West Yorkshire must be doing their nuts.

I mean, it's actually here: *Wuthering Heights*. You can *actually visit* the place! Top that, Yorkshire Dales! In your face, North York Moors! *Top Withins*, it's called. It's just over there, beyond that hill. True, the building is nothing like the place in the book, and it's a ruin now, but it's very much the location Emily Brontë had in mind when she wrote *Wuthering Heights*. Or so they reckon. Her life-long friend Ellen Nussey said so, and she should have known. So that proves it. Case closed. You can walk there from the Brontë Parsonage at the top of Haworth Main Street, across the windswept, wuthering moor. Just like many thousands of Japanese tourists do every year—so many that there are signposts in Japanese. Just like Ted Hughes and Sylvia Plath did, inspiring poems by both. Sylvia, who wrote the better poem, was a talented draughtswoman, and made a wonderful sketch of the ruin. She was thrilled by the place. It's indescribably atmospheric. Or so they tell me. I've never actually been there, of course. That sort of guff is for the tourists.

The story's setting isn't the only misconception people seem to have about *Wuthering Heights*. Take Heathcliff, for example: the great romantic hero. *Really?* Only if you've never actually read the book. Heathcliff is an utter bastard. *Dark and brooding* might be sexy to some women—although you rarely see it sought in the lonely hearts columns—but Heathcliff takes *bitter and twisted* to a whole new level. A sociopath, they would call him these days. A control freak. A man with serious anger-management issues. He hangs a spaniel, for Pete's sake! *Easy-going, with a GSOH*, Heathcliff most definitely is not.

The fact that so many people see *Wuthering Heights* as a romance frankly astonishes me. It's not a romance; it's a train-wreck. A highly enjoyable train-wreck, I'll grant you, but there's absolutely nothing in there to warm the cockles of your heart—unless you have something against spaniels. I more than half suspect most people's impressions of *Wuthering Heights* were formed through not listening closely enough to the lyrics of Kate Bush's song. Listen again: (SPOILER ALERT) the woman trying to get in through Heathcliff's window is *dead!* She's a *ghost*. Read the book: Cathy's body lies in the corner of a graveyard, surrounded by bilberry bushes. Yes, *bilberry bushes*. How West Yorkshire are those? You won't find many bilberries growing in the alkaline soils of the Yorkshire Dales!

Am I being overly precious about *Wuthering Heights* and the Brontës? Definitely. But look at it this way: there are literally scores of places in Yorkshire—yes, *Yorkshire*—associated with Robin Hood. Robin Hood's Bay, for example. And the great boulder named after him slap bang in the middle of the Moor: *Robin Hood's Penny Stone*. He's even supposed to have been born in Yorkshire (Barnsdale), and to be buried just fifteen miles from here, next to the River Calder, where his final arrow landed, fired from his deathbed in Kirklees Priory. Not that Robin Hood actually existed, you understand. But do the Yorkshire folk kick up a fuss when the good people of Nottinghamshire claim the man in Lincoln green and his *merrie men* all for their own? And even name their airport after him? Well, yes, I suppose they do. But good luck to Nottinghamshire: Robin Hood is one of their brands. Just as the Brontës are one of West Yorkshire's. Our gritstone landscape might not lend itself to tourist-friendly boxes of fudge, but the Brontë lasses certainly do.

Not that I'm entirely happy with this area's being thought of as *Brontë Country*. Yes, Haworth and the surrounding moors rightly lay claim to the Brontës, but Haworth is way over that way, seven miles up the old turnpike over the tops, not this neck of the moors at all.

But that's the big problem. How should you refer to this part of England, this stretch of the Pennines between the Peak District and the Yorkshire Dales? The Ordnance Survey maps refer to round here as the *South Pennines*. But that's crazy. We're on the twelfth thoracic vertebra of the Pennine backbone; if you're looking for the true South Pennines, the *coccyx* so to speak, that's way down somewhere near Edale in Derbyshire, not far from Sheffield in South Yorkshire. If the West Yorkshire Pennines are the South Pennines, what, pray, are the South Yorkshire Pennines? Don't they think about these things when they come up with these ridiculous names?

This place has an identity crisis. It almost seems to be defined by what it isn't. It's not the *Yorkshire Dales*, and it's not the *Peak District*, and it's bigger than just *Brontë Country* (genuine *Brontë Country*, that is), and nobody would ever guess it's supposed to be the *South Pennines*. How can you market an area when it doesn't even have a meaningful label? Holmfirth is *'Last of the Summer Wine' Country*; Mytholmroyd is *Ted Hughes Country*; Hebden Bridge is *Hippy Central* and *the Sapphic capital of Britain*; and Haworth is *Brontë Country* and *the place they filmed 'The Railway Children'*. Are we diluting our brand? Do we even have a brand to dilute? The high lands between the Peak District and the Yorkshire Dales have certain things in common, things which unite them. The millstone grit and the moors, for example. But we have no way of referring to them as a group, as a single entity. Which means they have an image problem, as well as an identity problem. Which means people confuse them with other places. Places which *do* have identities and names. Places like the Yorkshire Dales.

So, how should we refer to them, these in-between places that don't have a name? I'd like to call them the *West Yorkshire Moors*, but that would be to invite confusion with the *North York Moors*, which people often refer to simply, and incorrectly, as "the Yorkshire Moors". The *West Pennines* would be a good name, were it not for the fact that it's already used to describe the moors in Lancashire and Greater Manchester—how dare they! The *West Yorkshire Pennines* would be better, but would still be confused with the *West Pennines*. In the Derbyshire Peak District, they make a distinction between the millstone grit and limestone areas by referring to the *Dark Peak* and the *White Peak*. Perhaps West and North Yorkshire should do the same. Perhaps we could become the *Dark Dales*, in contrast with North Yorkshire's *White Dales*. But they would probably say we were trying to encroach on to their turf. The *Dark Moors*, then? No, not tourist-friendly, and it could easily be misheard as *Dartmoor. Millstone Country*? Yes, but the *Dark Peak* would rightly object: they have millstone grit too. *Milltown Country*? No, an oxymoron, and, heaven forbid, we would have to include parts of Lancashire! *The Wuthering Moors*, then? Do me a favour!

And then the Moor works its magic on me once again, and I realise that none of this matters. Who cares if some *Observer* journalist down south in London near Cornwall doesn't know her West from her North? And who cares if people think the Brontës lived in the Dales? And who cares if they think the South Pennines are in Derbyshire? So what if we're the best-kept secret in England? And so what if not many people come up here to visit? Why not keep it that way? Why not keep this wonderful place a secret all to ourselves? All the more for us!

All the more for me!

(No pun intended.)

Snow

Maundy Thursday, early April. I'm supposed to be writing, but Jen sent me a text message as she arrived at work this morning: "Fabulous day for a walk. Get on them hills." What more excuse did I need?

A fortnight ago, the two of us were paddling on a Northumberland beach, watching Geordie lads surfing: *Whey-aye Five-O!* Last week was more like June than the end of March: monthly heat records set on consecutive days in Scotland; hosepipe bans announced in the South East and, more to the point, most of Yorkshire. Last Sunday, I sat on the garden bench under our kitchen window, soaking up the sun. Bumble-bees and butterflies buzzed and fluttered around the garden in search of pollen, nectar and procreation. Male chaffinches battered the living daylights out of each other in vicious, claw-to-claw aerial combat. One of them even tried to take on his own reflection in the study window. The blue tits were in and out of the nestbox like creatures possessed. Spring had most definitely sprung. Or so we all thought.

Two-and-a-half days later, the night before last, a gale from the east brought four inches of snow, blocking roads and bringing down power-lines. I don't know what the winter equivalent of an Indian summer is called, but we were experiencing one. Fortunately, the thaw began almost immediately. By the end of yesterday, most of the snow in the valley had melted, although the surrounding moors were still predominantly white. Today dawned crisp and bright. Hence Jen's text message.

I climb the stile at the top of the field and jump down on to the Moor, landing in a shallow drift of snow. I've decided to follow my usual route in reverse today. Not for any aesthetic reason, but because I was feeling lazy and drove up as far as Nook Cottages to avoid the long slog up the road. I'm still slightly unnerved by my encounter with a lone sheep at the bottom of the field a couple of minutes ago. The poor creature bravely stood her ground as I approached. At first I didn't notice the lamb lying sodden and lifeless at her feet. Out of respect, I gave her a wide berth. Snow is the bane of lambing season.

There's a deep drift alongside the wall, but, just a metre or so away, it's already patchy. I decide to follow my usual path, buried somewhere beneath the drift. That was the whole point of coming up here: to get some snow-time.

Somebody else has already passed this way, but in the opposite direction. Deep footprints show me the way. I follow them, stepping into each one in turn. Walking in someone else's footprints makes the going a lot easier, even if it is sort of cheating. It's a technique that also works on sand, as I demonstrated to Jen while we were walking barefoot on the beach the other week. Compacted snow or sand gives you a firmer surface on which to walk; the pressure of your own feet compacts it further. Sheltered from the sun at the bottom of each shin-deep footprint, and denser than the surrounding snow due to the double-compaction, the snow beneath each of my footsteps should take longer to thaw, eventually leaving a trail of slushy footmarks on the track. That time might not be too far away: I wouldn't be surprised if most of this snow has melted by the end of the day. Jen was right, it really is fabulous.

A lapwing swoops and tumbles in courtship above the field to my left, its unearthly, arcade-game call like no other bird's. Definitely one of my top ten.

Bizarre! The footprints I'm following suddenly stop a few metres ahead. How can this be? Did my unknown predecessor materialise out of nowhere before heading down the track towards me? I'm genuinely perplexed. I trudge through the deepening drift to investigate. Mystery solved: whoever it was must have jumped down from the bank to my right—the bank that I must now climb. This is going to be quite diffic…

CRRUUUUNNNNCHHH!!! The snow gives way beneath my feet. I plunge through, all the way to my undercarriage. This is ridiculous! Each of my legs is trapped snugly in its own snowy well. I can't move. I look around to check nobody's watching. This is ridiculous!

What to do? I try lifting my right leg, but the snow encasing it prevents me from bending my knee. It's the same with my left. All joking aside, how am I going to get out of here? Start digging with my hands, I suppose. But then I have a brainwave, and let myself fall backwards. The weight of my body enlarges the leg-holes, allowing my knees to bend. I end up sitting in the snow drift. Then it's 'simply' a matter of extracting my legs from their holes, rolling on to my side, and flumping inelegantly to safety, like a walrus heading back to sea. I'm glad nobody's watching.

Having regained firmer ground—by which, I mean firmer snow—I continue along the drift, plunging down to my knees every five metres or so. I'm beginning to appreciate why they invented those ridiculous snow-shoes: it's surprisingly hard-going without them. Eventually, I reach the end of the wall and turn uphill. There's still plenty of snow up here, but, away from the wall, the drifts are nowhere near as deep.

I'm no longer following in my predecessor's footsteps, but am joined by others. Rabbit and grouse tracks weave intricate patterns in the snow. I'm delighted they've chosen to join me, my timid, time-shifted companions.

Rabbit tracks: two small, round prints in quick succession, then a pair of large, elongated prints side-by-side, then a gap, then the pattern repeated. The small prints are the front paws landing after a hop—one, two—then the large, rear feet overtake them, push down into the snow together—three/four—and the rabbit hops once more, over the gap to the next set of prints.

Grouse tracks: arrow-shaped, running in long, determined lines, pointing back the way they came. Side on, some of them take on the shape of birds in flight: self-portraits, almost. Feet in the shape of their owners. Fractal images in the fractal snow.

A pair of curlews pipe overhead as I near the end of the climb. The snow is even firmer up here. Legolas-like, I skip across it for a whole ten metres before unceremoniously plunging back through, although now it's only shin-deep once again. Turning right, I head along the edge towards the trig point. On the track, snow gives way in places to frozen puddles. Sinuous cracks within the ice map the contours of each small pool. Who would imagine how beautiful a frozen, muddy puddle can look? So beautiful, I try to avoid treading on them— although the pressure of my feet passing nearby occasionally sends compression waves through the mud, causing the ice to splinter like ancient glass.

A lone grouse explodes out of the heather, startling the life out of me: *HUU-UUU-UUU-URRR-RRR!* Stupid! Bloody! Grouse! It heads off towards the trig point in a hail of *guks*. I begin to regain my composure. There are dozens of grouse tracks up here. Many of them have indistinct marks trailing behind them, caused, I presume, by the insulating feathers on their feet brushing across the snow. Downy feet will come in handy in this weather.

I reach the trig point and touch it to make it official. It's getting even warmer now. A male skylark rises incongruously above me, singing for all he's worth. Anyone might think it was springtime. Skylarks and snow: you have to love the British weather!

Having taken in the view, I head on past the disused quarries and down the track through the heather. A grouse flap-glides against the snow far below. I decide to take a shortcut back to the stile, veering off the track to my right. Bad move: it proves impossible to judge the varying depths of snow between the clumps of heather. I stumble several times, causing anxiety for my bad ankle. I can't believe I forgot to bring my walking-stick: an invaluable piece of equipment for assessing snow depth. Meadow pipits flit about nervously, unsure what to do about the breathless buffoon flailing towards them. It would have been far quicker if I'd stuck to the track. Short cuts make long delays.

After what seems like an age, I reach the bottom of the slope. I jump off the bank on to the track and fall flat on my face, making a neat, Richard-shaped hole in the snow. I rise spluttering and laughing. I don't care if anybody was watching this time. That was fun.

I'm back at the wall with its snowdrift. Turning north, I walk alongside it for three- or four-hundred metres, until I reach the stile. I climb on top, and take in the view once more. Yes, Jen was right—as ever.

I turn to climb back down into the field. Fifty metres ahead of me, the lone sheep is where I left her. I'd forgotten all about her. And then I see it: a tiny lamb, suckling hungrily between her legs, wagging its tail like some demented spaniel. You idiot, Carter! That bedraggled lump wasn't lifeless; it had only just been born!

Drumming

An early morning in June, just below the trig point. I'm standing in the heather at the edge of one of the disused gritstone quarries, looking west towards Heptonstall. Hebden Bridge lies hidden in the valley below.

I should come up here at this time of day more often. With the sun to my back, the familiar shadows across the valley have yet to form. Everything is illuminated: the woods at Hardcastle Crags; the 'bride stones' of Bridestones Moor; and Pendle Hill, just visible through the gap above Widdop reservoir. I'm seeing my world in a whole new light.

It's quieter at this time of day too. The world is still waking. Nobody has had time to mess things up. I have the Moor all to myself.

And then the noise begins. Over the brow of the hill, a plasticky, vibrato horn calls out; an eerie, ululating kazoo. It last for five seconds or so, there's a pause, then it repeats—and repeats again. Bizarre. It's getting louder. What the hell is it? Has some soccer hooligan brought their vuvuzela up here for a spot of practise?

We'll be having words. But no, it's mellower than that—electronic almost. Synth music on the Moor: is nothing sacred?

The commotion continues to grow. I should be able to see what's causing it by now. The sound is zipping back and forth so quickly, it must be very close indeed. It's almost on top of me.

And then I look up.

A small, long-billed bird beats rapidly up into the sky, reaches its summit, and enters into a steep and graceful curving dive. The haunting drone fills the air, then cuts as the bird pulls out of the dive. I watch, open-mouthed, as the creature roller-coasts to a new summit, then drops into another Stuka dive, its Jericho trumpet blasting forth.

After all these years, I'm finally witnessing the famous courtship display of a snipe.

I've encountered snipe on the Moor before, although not as often as you might expect. They tend to keep well-hidden, relying on their superb mottled-brown camouflage for protection. All my previous snipe encounters have been very short-lived, as they flushed from the moor-grass directly at my feet and flew off high and fast, jinking to left and right, emitting their panicky *scaap! scaap!* call (usually accompanied by a panicky, bellowed *HUU-UUU-UUU-URRR-RRR!* call of my own).

The snipe's habit of flushing late and taking evasive manoeuvres as it flees makes it a particularly challenging game bird for those intent on blasting such creatures out of the sky. "How well I remember killing my first snipe," an elderly Charles Darwin reminisced about his misspent youth, "…my excitement was so great that I had much difficulty in reloading my gun from the trembling of my hands." Darwin also used to tell how, during the *Beagle* voyage, he had killed twenty-three snipe in twenty-four shots—but, modest to a fault, was always at pains to add that South American snipe were probably not quite so wild as their British cousins.

I watch as the bird crests another summit and heads into its next dive: *wu-wu-wu-wu-wu-wu-wu-wu-wu-wuu-wuu-wUUUUUUw!* It's a noise that earned the snipe many a goatish nickname: *heather-bleater* in Scotland; *gabharín reo* ('little goat of the frost') in Gaelic; *taivaanvuohi* ('sky goat') in Finnish.

The *drumming* noise of the snipe receives an honourable mention in Darwin's *The Descent of Man and Selection in Relation to Sex*:

> *The drumming, or bleating, or neighing, or thundering noise, as expressed by different observers, which is made by the common snipe… must have surprised every one who has ever heard it. This bird, during the pairing-season, flies to "perhaps a thousand feet in height," and after zig-zagging about for a time descends in a curved line, with outspread tail and quivering pinions, with surprising velocity to the earth. The sound is emitted only during this rapid descent.*

Darwin goes on to credit Mr Meves, the Conservator at

the zoological museum in Stockholm, with first correctly identifying the source of the snipe's drumming noise. In a paper, which appeared in translation in 1858 in the *Proceedings of the Zoological Society of London*, Meves outlined previous hypotheses about the source of the drumming noise, before giving his own observations:

> *Bechstein thought that it was produced by means of the beak; Naumann and others, again, that it originated in powerful strokes of the wing: but since Pralle in Hanover observed that the bird makes heard its well-known song or cry, which he expressed with the words "gick jack, gick jack!" at the same time with the neighing sound, it seemed to be settled that this latter is not produced through the throat. In the mean time I have remarked with surprise, that the humming sound could never be observed whilst the bird was flying upwards, at which time the tail is closed; but only when it was casting itself downwards in a slanting direction, with the tail strongly spread out.*

Meves goes on to suggest that the source of the snipe's drumming noise is its long, sabre-shaped outer tail-feathers. He then describes having verified his hypothesis by attaching a snipe's tail-feather to the end of a stick and waving it around his head, thereby successfully reproducing the enigmatic sound.

152 years later, in 2010, a team of scientists from Manchester also investigated the 'sonation' of male snipe—initially, through the not entirely original method of attaching some tail-feathers to a stick and waving it about. They then moved on to more

sophisticated apparatus, including a hair-dryer, high-speed video camera, digital audio-processing software, and a borrowed wind-tunnel. They found that the extended trailing halves of the snipe's outer tail-feathers each contain a hinge-like feature running along their length. These hinges allow the feathers, powered by a process known as *vortex shedding*, to flap rapidly back and forth during the snipe's dive, like flags in a strong wind. It is this flapping that causes the characteristic *drumming* noise.

I can't help thinking this simple hinge adaptation—a slight weakness in the feathers, caused by the adjacent barbs' not hooking together at that point—would have delighted a certain Mr Darwin.

Darwin coined the phrase *Sexual Selection* to describe what takes place when individuals of a particular species compete for access to mates—be it through trying to attract members of the opposite sex, or to ward-off would-be sexual competitors. Sexual Selection is really just a special case of Natural Selection in action: attracting and keeping a mate can be every bit as important in passing on your genes to future generations as avoiding predators, surviving in adverse conditions, and obtaining sufficient food.

Sexual Selection, like Natural Selection in general, is a major driver in the evolution of species, often resulting in some pretty bizarre contrivances. When it comes to attracting members of the opposite sex, there is often no accounting for taste. The classic example is the peacock's tail, the mere sight of which, Darwin confessed to an American friend, made him feel sick. No male bird in his right mind would choose to be burdened with such an outlandish appendage. Indeed, its very presence seems to run contrary to normal Darwinian Natural Selection: having such a flamboyant tail is bound to be disadvantageous to the male in terms of evading detection and capture by predators. So why hasn't Natural Selection winnowed out such an abhorrence? The answer seems to be that, for whatever reason, the female birds, the peahens, find flamboyant tails a major turn-on. So any over-endowed male is likely to have more success with the ladies and bear more offspring. Furthermore, any male offspring from such unions are likely to inherit their father's genes for more flamboyant tails, and any female offspring are more likely to inherit their mother's preference for such tails. So, over the generations, female preference will reward the evolution of ever more flamboyant male tails. But only up to a point. Eventually, the flamboyant tails become such a burden that normal Natural Selection kicks in, preventing them from becoming any more over-the-top. The peacock's tail, for all its apparent profligacy, is a subtle compromise; a trade-off between two opposing selective pressures: to attract members of the opposite sex, and to avoid being eaten.

But why would a peahen have such a preference for flamboyant tails? It might have started as a genetic whim: some random predilection that got out of hand. Or perhaps a natural inclination to identify males of their own species by looking at their tails was also seized upon by Sexual Selection with outlandish results. Or perhaps flamboyant tails indicate 'better' suitors in some way. For example, being able to survive with such an unwieldy encumbrance could indicate that the male bird has got what it takes to survive, so would make an excellent father. Or perhaps some combination of these and other reasons. *Evolutionary Just-So stories:* take your pick. The reason for such preferences doesn't really matter. All Sexual Selection needs to get to work is for there to be a preference in the first place.

Five minutes have passed, and the snipe is still roller-coasting. There's no sign of any females, but for all I know there are dozens of them watching from the hidden safety of the moor-grass. Good luck to him! Courting the ladies with your musical tail-feathers might seem like an odd approach, but is it any more weird than a male grouse trying to woo them with his ridiculous eyebrows, or some fat cat with his ridiculous Ferrari?

Whatever rocks your boat.

On the Level

A blustery, damp November afternoon. Overcast. Nondescript. A perfect day for staying indoors, lighting a fire, and watching a crappy old film on the telly. A day for toast, and a few too many mugs of tea. Only a complete idiot would be caught outside on a day like today.

I gaze across the flat, monochrome expanse, thinking of Thomas Hood's poem:

> *No sun—no moon!*
> *No morn—no noon!*
> *No dawn—no dusk—no proper time of day...*
> *November!*

The heather is as drab as the dawn, the horizon vague and indeterminate. Nimbostratus six shades of grey shifts and overlaps, drifting up and across, heading east. The wind is picking up. Rain threatens, but rain has been threatening all day.

I think my right boot might be about to leak. They've

been good boots—eighteen years, countless miles—but there can't be many walks left in them. Entropy will have her way. The boots slide, heavy with mud. Idiot mountain bikers have been churning up the track again.

Tear-salt stings my left eye—my windward eye. Random gusts collar-clout my ears. Specks of unidentified botanical jetsam near-miss my face. I wouldn't have it any other way. It's November: this is what November is *supposed* to be like. You think this is dank and miserable? You should come back in February.

My lungs thrill, their capacity miraculously expanded. Bigger lungs take longer to fill, my breathing slows, I breathe deeper still. There is only one cliché for it: *bracing*. Skegness: now there was a place that knew how to sell you the wind. Spin before spin was invented. Why *suffolkate* in Southwold, when you could be leaping in Lincolnshire with a fat, jolly fisherman?

This wind will be blowing off the east coast shortly, on its way to Denmark and beyond. Wherever is beyond. But not to worry, there seems to be plenty more wind where that came from, coasting over the tops from the Irish Sea.

I blink. Perhaps it's not tear-salt after all. Perhaps it's the Atlantic.

Am I perverse? Why do I love this place so much, this flat, often bleak, nothing-but-heather moor? What makes it so special, even on days like this? Perhaps especially on days like this.

Obviously, one reason I keep trudging up here is because it's on my doorstep: fifteen minutes' walk from home, and I can be on the Moor; twenty minutes' walk, and I can be in the middle of nowhere. Part of the Moor's appeal is undoubtedly its convenience. Like all successful organisms, I've adapted to my environment; I've found my niche. If I lived near the woods, I would walk in the woods, claustrophobic though they might now seem. If I lived near the sea, I would walk near the sea, and would no doubt write a book about it. If I lived in London, well... I would have to move. You have to draw the line somewhere. I love Anglesey's rocky coast. I love the Yorkshire Dales. I love the woods, hedgerows, fields and marshes of my native Wirral. But, like all of them, the West Yorkshire moors are part of me now. I love the Moor, despite its bleak, heathery flatness. I love the Moor *because of* its bleak, heathery flatness. That's what makes it the Moor.

I wonder what it is that attracts me to bleak landscapes. Shetland must be partly to blame: those three unforgettable weeks I spent up there on an archaeological dig in 1985, digging in the bitter mud and snow; drinking in pubs run by landlords with lax interpretations of the licensing laws; acquiring a love for hitherto unappreciated folk music. As life-changing events go, it was up there. But then there is Anglesey, which can also be bleak when it puts its mind to it, and the west coast of Ireland. And not to forget the rugged Yorkshire Dales. I always preferred the Dales to the more celebrated, achingly beautiful but occasionally fudge-box twee Lake District. I guess my love of bleak landscapes is a northern and western thing. I'm pretty sure it must be possible to experience bleak down in Kent, the self-styled *Garden of England*, but it's hard to imagine.

I also love the Moor because it's so familiar. Whoever said familiarity breeds contempt was talking out of their arse. Familiarity breeds identity. Familiarity breeds deep comfort. I just don't understand the craving for new experiences all of the time. Why on earth not stick with what you know and love? *Munro-bagging*, I ask you! How can you ever claim to know a single Scottish mountain? Why, then, the trainspotteresque compulsion to *bag* all 283? Don't even get me started on fell-runners and mountain-bikers, who seem to see the countryside as some sort of challenge: something to conquer, rather than appreciate. Slow down, breathe deep, open your eyes, and pay attention. Become more familiar with the already familiar. Go for depth, not breadth. Go for malt, not blend.

How can you claim to be familiar with a place, if you haven't experienced it in all weathers, at all times of the year? The true delight in the familiar is knowing what to expect, and what's new or out of place. Like the first golden plover I saw on the Moor. I heard it long before I saw it, and knew immediately it was something new: its wheezing call just didn't fit. Seeing something new in a place you visit all the time makes it special, even though you might not think it special if you saw it somewhere else. Location is a major factor in the experience. That's why people reminisce about where they were when Kennedy was shot, or when they heard about 9/11. Either that, or they're sticking to their alibis.

But far more joyful to me than seeing something new in a familiar place, is seeing something familiar in a familiar place. Especially if it's something seasonal, something whose arrival I've been anticipating for months. The first early morning sighting of Orion over our gate in autumn. Snowdrops in early spring. Swallows in April. The first bats hunting above our patio. The first curlews, lapwings and wheatears on the Moor. Until you know what to expect, you don't know what to look out for—nor do you notice what's missing. Familiarity also breeds anticipation.

Then there's the flatness of the Moor. I love that too. In their observations on world travel, documented in the sleeve notes of their classic album *Stop Making Sense*, avant-garde rock band *Talking Heads* noted that people never travel to look at flat landscapes. This isn't entirely true, I went to Norfolk once, and to Holland, but I can see where they were coming from. People like rolling hills and majestic mountains. If they want level horizons, they go to the seaside. They go to Skegness.

Level is underrated. We don't celebrate it enough. People think level is flat and, well, boring. They're wrong. Tragically wrong.

For a landscape to be level, it must be large. You need a lot of space to give a flat horizon. Too much space to appreciate. Too much to depict on a box of fudge. The

American comedian Rich Hall, an occasional visitor to these parts, once said that, where he comes from in Montana, it's so flat that you can watch your dog run away for three days. Flat means big, empty, uninterrupted views, and even bigger skies. Flat means exposed. Flat means nowhere to hide, except in the largeness itself.

I love the Moor's sheer size. Large, flat expanses can be incredibly deceptive when it comes to scale. More than once, I've come up here with my friend the farmer to help bring her beef cattle down from the Moor for the winter. You would think that spotting a herd of cattle on a flat, empty moor would be a piece of cake. Think again. We spent ages looking for them one time. The Moor simply swallowed them in its vastness. My friend, with her farmer's eye for cattle, eventually spotted them. She pointed towards some empty piece of moorland and headed off, with me trailing behind. It took me another five minutes before I finally saw them. I'd been looking straight at them, but had the scale all wrong. I had been looking for something far bigger.

The Moor's marvellous flatness also means it has an immense sky: pretty much an entire hemisphere's worth. There was a girl with us on the Shetland dig who came from New York City. I don't think she had ever seen the sky before. Not properly, anyway. It freaked her out how we could tell it was going to rain—actually, no, make that *hail*—five minutes before the hail actually arrived. In the same way that I'm not used to looking for cattle on a moor, she wasn't used to looking to the sky to gauge the approaching weather. She didn't have the eye for it. In fairness to her, she probably wasn't used to having sky to look at. There are no such problems on the Moor: you can see rain and hail heading your way from miles off. The trouble is, there's little benefit in seeing them coming, as there's absolutely nowhere to shelter. Experience has taught me that the best way to deal with hail when you're caught in the open is to turn your back to it, stand still, and wait for it to go away. Unfortunately, the same trick doesn't seem to work on any people you might spot approaching on an intercept course, intent on spoiling your solitude. The best course of action there is to change direction. You'll have plenty of advance warning, vertical humans' being far easier to spot in flat landscapes than horizontal cattle.

The big-sky view westward from the Moor can be stunning in changeable weather. I've never known a place like it for *crepuscular rays*: those dramatic beams of light that seem to spread fan-like through the clouds from the Sun. As they're to the west, the drama is accentuated by having Stoodley Pike Monument in the background—or in the foreground, depending on how you look at these things. *Divine light*, some people call it, hopefully tongue-in-cheek: shifting beams' spotlighting the fields on the hillsides opposite, turning them momentarily emerald.

Flat landscape's very bigness is its big problem. Flat landscape is undervalued because it's so big. There's so much of it, what possible harm could there be in losing some? Look at all that sea not doing anything! Let's drill for gas! Look at that huge moor going to waste! Let's put up a pile of wind turbines! Look at all that desert! It's just crying out for solar panels! So what if the ice-caps are melting? There's plenty more ice in the Arctic!

In the same way that people never travel to look at flat landscapes, they seldom seem to kick up a fuss when flat landscapes are threatened. Those who do are accused of *nimbyism*: an odious word in more ways than one. In the last few years, I've seen the north west horizon of the gloriously flat Dee Marshes on the Wirral defiled by gas rig and wind turbine. Similar turbines now also mar the seascapes of my beloved Anglesey. Even Skegness hasn't escaped the cancer, with yet another wind power-station belittling its once-bracing scenery. One day soon, no doubt, the Moor will be surrounded by—and quite possibly covered in—yet more of these impotent, flailing forests of distraction. Another horizontal landscape will have been verticalised, another horizon diminished. Claustrophobia will have come to yet another former open space.

Some people claim to like the look of these monstrosities. Some even go so far as to claim they somehow *enhance* the landscape. The kind of people, presumably, who think that candles enhance a cake. These people have been sold the wind. They've fallen for the spin. The sort of spin that turns power-stations into *farms*, megawatts into *heated homes*, and glorified pre-industrial technology into a realistic solution to the desperate problem of twenty-first century global carbon emissions. They seem to forget that there are seven-billion other people out there on this tiny planet. We need serious solutions to serious problems. To put it frankly, we need nuclear power.

I fasten my collar. The air tastes of approaching winter. Raising a finger to the turbines on the skyline, I head off into the expanse, disappearing into the bigness.

Shafts

It's such an *un-Octoberish* October day that I've decided to take an excursion, to revisit three of my former haunts from the *Old Moor Walk*. Blue sky and fluffy stratocumulus clouds' notwithstanding, the track across the expanse is a quagmire. The passage of feet over the years has lowered the track several centimetres below the general lie of the land. Water always finds its own level: it seeps down on to the track from either side, creating shining puddles in the peaty blackness. To stop the erosion getting worse, you're supposed to stick to the track in conditions like these, but my feet are already wet enough, and the mud is treacherous. So I walk alongside the track, hopping from one side to the other, picking my grassy tussocks and heather clumps with care.

Despite my general hopelessness at plant identification, one thing I have learnt during my countless walks on the Moor is that, at this time of year, large areas of rust-coloured cotton-grass signal bog. There are many such patches up ahead. Perhaps heading this way in October wasn't such a bright idea after all. But it's kind of fun, and the closest I'm likely to get to an adventure these days.

Although I keep going on about the flatness of the terrain up here, the flatness is on a wide scale. The whole area is a plateau, so, when you're on the tops, the horizon looks very flat indeed. But, on a more local scale—on the scale of the Moor—the flatness is broken into levels, reflecting different geological strata and fault-line discontinuities. The area that I refer to as *the expanse*, which the maps call *Dimmin Dale*, is indeed large and flat, sloping gently towards the east. But there are higher levels to the south (from where I've just descended) and to the north. Hence, I suppose, this area's being described as a 'dale', even though it doesn't look, or feel, remotely like a valley. But the lie of the land means water tends to drain into the expanse from the higher land to the north and south—which explains the bogs.

I reach my first rusty patch. As expected, the peat here is mostly underwater. There's no way I can cross it without getting extremely wet. So I make a wide detour, and then another. This is going to be slow going.

All of the moors around here form a huge water-catchment area. But the spongy nature of the bogs means you tend not to come across many streams until you head down into the valleys. The water just seeps out. Although it's located close to the western edge of the Pennines, the Moor is on the eastern side of the Pennine watershed. All of the water draining from this bog will eventually flow under the Humber Bridge and into the North Sea.

I'm nearly through the bog, but a final, huge, waterlogged patch blocks my way. This is crazy. Dry land is no more than fifteen metres away, but I can't figure out how to get there. I can hear running water. There must be a spring nearby. I decide to skirt the wet patch, heading up the gentle slope in search of drier ground. In so doing, I almost step into the spring. Crystal-clear water babbles up out of the ground between two large tussocks, and immediately dissipates into the rusty grass. Might this be the world's shortest river?

Dry land at last! I climb on to the low terrace of rocks that has been my planned destination all along. It's not a natural terrace: human beings dumped and levelled these rocks, a spoil-heap. On top of the terrace sits a small, flat-topped, circular, stone structure with four cast-iron grilled windows: the top of an air-shaft.

These shafts intrigued me for years. There are three of them on the Moor, and I know of a couple of others beyond the Moor to the east. The three up here, of which this shaft is the easternmost, were built in a perfectly straight line, pointing just north of west from here. I can see the middle shaft on the skyline, on its own excavated terrace. The western shaft is over the brow of the hill and lower down. For years, I thought these shafts must ventilate some sort of mine. If you extend their line westwards, it points directly at the nearby settlement of Pecket Well, located high on the valley side just below the Moor. It seemed obvious to me that some sort of drift mine must have been dug from there into the side of the valley, running more or less horizontally in a straight line under the Moor. The absence of any sign of a mine entrance at Pecket Well was, therefore, somewhat perplexing. It was with considerable nerdy delight that I recently learnt of the shafts' true purpose, and of their tenuous link with my hero, Charles Darwin. Mind you, when you're a true Darwin groupie, pretty much everything has a Darwin connection.

One of the air-shaft's window-grilles has been removed and is propped against the stonework. This is a listed building, I wonder who will repair it. As always, I circle round to the lea side of the building and listen intently at the nearest window. It takes a few seconds for my hearing to adjust. Yes, there it is: *white noise!* But is it the sound of wind or water I can hear coming up the shaft? I've never been entirely sure before, but today I'm in no doubt: it's clearly water.

A pair of grouse explode out of the heather right in front of me: *HUU-UUU-UUU-URRR-RRR! Guk———— guk————— guk————— guk———— guk———— guk—— guk— guk!* After my heart has stopped pounding, I head up the slope towards the middle air-shaft, along a proper, dryish footpath. The second shaft is pretty much identical to the first. Again, I walk around it, listening for water. But this time I can't hear any. Perhaps it's because I'm higher up, farther from the water.

I'm near the top of the slope now, just a stone's throw from the flat summit with the unlikely name of Tom Tittiman. But, as there's no trig point to make my ascent official, I continue along the footpath to the steep edge of the hill. From here, I look down on the third air-shaft, located next to a ruined farmhouse. Beyond the air-shaft, the Moor gives way to fields. Beyond the fields, I can just make out a few of the rooftops at Pecket Well. Beyond the rooftops, there's the steep valley of Middle Dean, then more hillside fields, a hidden valley, more moorland, and, finally, almost five miles away, the long grassy dam of Widdop Reservoir.

Widdop Reservoir, it turns out, is what the air-shafts are all about. They provide ventilation to one of a series of underground conduits channelling water from Widdop and a couple of the other local reservoirs to the Albert Water-Treatment Works on the outskirts of Halifax, almost five miles behind me.

In his poem about Widdop Reservoir, Ted Hughes observed that where there had previously been nothing, somebody had put a lake. The *somebody* in question was a local lad from near Halifax, one John Frederic Bateman. Bateman spent almost his entire career designing and constructing reservoirs and waterworks throughout Britain and farther afield. His crowning achievement was a series of reservoirs in the Peak District to supply water to the City of Manchester. The water, which first reached the city in 1851, was supplied via an eighteen-mile, gravity-fed, underground aqueduct. Bateman preferred, wherever practicable, to rely on gravitational systems, rather than steam-powered water-pumps. His conduit beneath the Moor is a similar gravity-fed system, feeding water from Widdop Reservoir (320 metres above sea-level) to the water-works in Halifax (250 metres above sea-level)—albeit via an aqueduct-bridge across Crimsworth Dean Beck in the valley below (only 160 metres above sea-level). Water always finds its own level: the aqueduct beneath the Moor is a glorified, nine-mile-long siphon.

It would be difficult to overestimate the importance of John Bateman's work. He was one of the great engineers of the nineteenth century, providing clean drinking-, washing- and steam-engine-water to the ever-burgeoning northern towns and cities driving the Industrial Revolution. When Manchester's demand for water outgrew even his Peak District reservoirs, Bateman suggested, and provided expert advice to, an ambitious project to create a new lake in Cumbria,

Thirlmere, which would supply water to the city via a one-hundred-mile-long aqueduct.

For some reason, water- and sewage-treatment systems—vitally important civil-engineering works—never seem to derive quite the same *kudos* as the construction of new bridges and railways. Perhaps this is one reason why, in 1869, Bateman and a colleague wrote a paper entitled *Channel Railway: Description of a Proposed Cast-Iron Tube for Carrying a Railway Across the Channel Between the Coasts of England and France*. The proposal, needless to say, never got off the ground—nor under the sea. But, *kudos* notwithstanding, Bateman did very well for himself designing and building great waterworks. So much so that he was eventually able to buy the magnificent Moor Park country estate near Farnham in Surrey. I hasten to point out that there are no moors in Surrey: the estate was named after a previous owner's previous estate, the name of which was a corruption of the former Manor of More in Hertfordshire.

The gentleman who sold Moor Park to Bateman was another man whose business might be described as *water-treatment*: Edward Wickstead Lane. Lane was one of numerous practitioners of the faddish *water cure*, also known as *hydropathy*: a quack medical discipline used to treat all manner of ailments. Patients were made to take cold showers and steam-baths, wrap themselves in wet towels, and drink lots of water. As quack treatments go, it was relatively harmless, apart from increased risk of catching pneumonia or drowning. As with so many other quack treatments, hydropathy was perceived to work by many of the people who underwent it: the *placebo effect* in action. Indeed, undergoing such treatment might well have done some patients genuine good, as it also tended to involve changes in diet, abstinence from mental activity, and taking long, relaxing walks in the countryside—a form of therapy I heartily endorse.

Edward Lane's most famous patient at his Moor Park hydropathy establishment was a certain Charles Darwin. Shortly after his return to Britain, following his five-year voyage around the world aboard *HMS Beagle*, Darwin began to be afflicted by numerous, strange medical symptoms. They continued to affect him, with varying degrees of intensity, for the rest of his life. The symptoms included: extreme spasmodic flatulence; excessive saliva secretions; acidic vomiting; shivering; hysterical crying; dying sensations; copious, pallid urine; ringing in the ears; black dots before the eyes; heart palpitations; nervousness; a crimson, ulcerated tongue; extreme tiredness; eczema; lumbago; and plenty more besides. To this day, nobody is at all sure what ailed Charles Darwin. For what it's worth, my hunch is that not all of his symptoms were related, and that he was afflicted by more than one medical condition. All manner of retrospective diagnoses have been suggested: from *Chaghas Disease* caught, perhaps, from an insect bite in South America, to arsenic poisoning; from myalgic encephalomyelitis (ME), to *Crohn's Disease*; from some sort of psycho-somatic illness, to 'chronic fatigue syndrome'. Some people have even suggested Darwin's ailments were no more than a convenient excuse to avoid attending scientific meetings and social functions, although it's clear from his personal records and correspondence that his symptoms were genuine—as was the distress they caused. Of no minor embarrassment to Darwin was his flatulence. Imagine my childish delight, therefore, many years ago, when I worked out that Darwin's full name, Charles Robert Darwin, is an anagram of *rectal winds abhorrer*.

Darwin first visited Moor Park in 1857, but that was by no means the first time he took the water cure. He had, on numerous previous occasions, attended a similar establishment run by Dr James Gully in Malvern. Despite his initial scepticism, Darwin had become convinced that hydropathy was effective in alleviating some of his symptoms—although he had no time at all for other quack practices endorsed by Gully, such as homeopathy, mesmerism, and clairvoyance. Indeed, so convinced was Darwin of the efficacy of the water cure that, when his favourite child, his daughter Annie, was taken seriously ill, he whisked her off to Malvern in a fit of desperation. It was to no avail: Annie died in Malvern, aged ten, on 23rd April 1851. In the absence of genuine therapies, placebo treatments sometimes turn out to be not quite so harmless after all. Darwin was devastated. He rushed home to comfort his heavily pregnant wife, missed Annie's funeral, and couldn't bring himself to visit her grave for many years.

The events surrounding Annie's illness and death, while Darwin was working on his as-yet-unpublished theory of evolution, are portrayed in the 2009 film *Creation*. It's a real curate's egg of a film: Paul Bettany is perfect as Charles Darwin; the future Sherlock Holmes (and Smaug the Dragon), Benedict Cumberbatch, is equally perfect as Joseph Dalton Hooker; many of the film's details are spot-on; but please, whatever you do, don't be taken in by any of the nonsense where Darwin imagines seeing dead animals coming back to life, and chases Annie's ghost through the streets of Malvern: nothing remotely like either event ever happened.

The loss of his beloved daughter left Darwin with painful memories of Malvern. Moor Park, being much closer to his home in Kent, eventually provided a more attractive alternative.

Darwin seems to have enjoyed his stays at Moor Park, flirting with young lady guests, taking up billiards, and going for walks on the estate and in the surrounding countryside. During his first visit, he wrote to Hooker:

> *I am undergoing hydropathy for a fortnight, having been here a week, and having already received an amount of good which is quite incredible to myself and quite unaccountable. I can walk and eat like a hearty Christian, and even my nights are good. I cannot in the least understand how hydropathy can act as it certainly does on me. It dulls one's brain splendidly; I have not thought about a single species of any kind since leaving home.*

He then immediately makes a liar of himself by asking

Hooker several questions about Alpine plant species.

But Moor Park proved far too lavish for Edward Lane's business needs. After a few years, he decided to up-sticks and move to more suitable premises in nearby Richmond. His decision to move might also have been influenced by a public scandal: Lane was being sued for adultery by the jealous husband of a woman whose diary recorded an illicit, quite possibly fantastical encounter with the doctor. Whatever the reason for his decision, Edward Lane sold Moor Park to John Bateman the water-engineer in 1859.

The sale of Moor Park left Darwin temporarily in the lurch. He was exhausted, having just put the finishing touches to the first edition of *On the Origin of Species*. An alternative hydropathic establishment needed to be found. Memories of Malvern were still too painful, so Darwin headed north for a couple of months, leaving for Wells House, Ilkley, on 2nd October 1859.

Which explains how it came to pass that Charles Darwin was taking the water cure on another Yorkshire gritstone moor, just thirteen miles across the tops from where I'm standing, on the day that the greatest book in the history of biology first appeared in print.

Skull

I turn from the trig point on High Brown Knoll and head back down the way I came, along Deer Stones Edge. I'm farther afield than usual today, making the most of the unseasonably warm February weather. Below me, the humps and bumps of the disused quarry on Delf End Flat twist and interweave like some giant, grass-covered Henry Moore sculpture. An elephants' graveyard, perhaps. Beyond the quarry, the obelisk war memorial on Smeakin Hill faces and echoes its bigger brother across the valley on Stoodley Pike.

Deer Stones Edge: as opposed to the nearby, far more familiar *Sheep Stones Edge*. I can see plenty of stones all right, but none of them reminds me of a deer. Mind you, how many other people would see an elephants' graveyard from up here?

I reach the end of the edge. A steep, deeply rutted track leads down towards the air-shaft and ruined farm below. I follow it for twenty metres or so, then break off to the left to skirt the delightfully named Bog Eggs Edge. Below the edge, the new owners of Bog Eggs Farm recently committed the unforgivable sin of renaming their residence. I'm guessing the old name wasn't deemed appropriate for their new equestrian centre. Angry letters have appeared in the *Hebden Bridge Times*. For once, I agree with the easily outraged: you shouldn't mess with names like that. This is how things are forgotten, how entropy wins. *Bog Eggs* says it all: the farm is situated on the edge of a bog. *Allswell Farm* has no history. It lacks heritage.

Something small and white catches my eye in the heather. I deviate from the track to investigate. What is this? Another Henry Moore sculpture? An exquisite alabaster maquette, perhaps? No, something more gruesome. Something to put the *skull* into *sculpture*. A cranium the size of my hand nestles amongst the heather roots on a bed of grey-brown fur and moss. A study in mortality.

I crouch closer. The skull has a raptorish look to it: those huge eye-sockets, and the beak-like nose. But this was no bird of prey. The fur and teeth are the obvious give-away, while the eye-sockets on the side of the head indicate prey, not predator. No, not a raptor; the former occupant of this skull was, without doubt, a bunny.

The skull has been picked clean. It must have lain here for some time. Long enough, at least, for green algae to have established themselves on some of the less-exposed surfaces. The two empty eye sockets stare up at me, emotionless, finally beyond fear. Beneath them, the nose bone has fallen away, revealing a long, heart-shaped nasal cavity. From the centre of this cavity, the joint between the two halves of the skull—the frontal suture—has begun to separate. A thin, dark crack runs up between the eye-sockets, across the forehead, and disappears over the back of the cranium. A similar crack runs down from the nasal cavity, dividing the dead rabbit's incisors. The rabbit skull has a hare-lip.

I suddenly find myself reminded of a long-forgotten poem we were made to learn at school, about the body of a dead knight found rotting in some undergrowth on a mountainside—a place not entirely unlike here. Unlike Auden's The Night Mail, Tennyson's The Eagle, and Edgar's "Come on, sir; here's the place…" speech from King Lear, only a couple of random phrases from John Masefield's poem have survived entropy in my brain: stuff about bones being bleached and blanched with the summer sun, the body dwindling to a skeleton, and straggling ivy twisting and creeping in eye sockets. Stirring stuff for any twelve-year-old boy to learn by heart, then entirely forget about. Those fragments of poetry have been hidden away in my brain somewhere for well over thirty years, waiting for a trigger like this. What else is in there I'm not remembering?

I wonder what killed the rabbit. A stoat? A dog? The myxoma virus? Old age? Foxes and buzzards take their fair share of rabbits, but, after centuries of persecution, these predators are relatively rare in grouse- and sheep-country. Whatever it was that killed the rabbit, I wouldn't mind betting that crows were involved in the clean-up operation. Crows and maggots. There's not a hint of raw flesh or meat remaining on the carcass. Nor, apart from the skull, do there appear to be any other bones. Perhaps the crows carried them away. Perhaps they're hidden amongst the tangled mass of fur. I'm certainly not prepared to investigate!

I find myself thinking back to the time at Durham University, when a local G.P. came to visit the archaeology department. In his spare time, he provided anatomical advice about archaeological finds. He also gave students hands-on tutorials involving human and animal bones. I astonished him by confidently (and correctly) guessing that the Anglo-Saxon human skull he had asked me to describe was female. He congratulated me, asking how I'd been able to tell, as sexing skulls is far from easy. I then pissed off every feminist in the group by joking that I'd noticed a lot of wear and tear around the jaw area: a sure-sign, I claimed, of incessant talking. My sins were soon forgotten, however, when the girl next to me threw the ancient human femur she had been examining across the table in horror, on learning that the large growth at one end was a sign of leprosy. Finally, we were given a cardboard box full of bones, challenged to lay them out on the table in the right order, then try to identify what manner of creature they once belonged to. We correctly identified our reassembled skeleton as that of a dog, despite having got its rib-cage the wrong way round.

Skulls and skeletons of different species are surprisingly difficult to tell apart—for non-experts at least. You're used to seeing fat, fluffy rabbits and woolly sheep, and suddenly you're looking at a pile of desiccated bones that might almost as easily have belonged to a hedgehog or a deer. Yes, you should be able to hone your guesses if you look a bit more closely—large canines, think carnivore; no upper incisors, think ungulate—but, under the skin, we're a lot more similar than we might think. Back in 1840, had Robert Fitch set a rabbit's skull alongside that of Sir Thomas Browne, recently *knav'd* from his grave, he would have noticed a number of striking similarities in the way the two, clearly very different skulls were structured. Like the rabbit's, Sir Thomas Browne's skull would have had a long, frontal suture, and a number of other sutures, joining the bones of the cranium together. Like the rabbit's, Sir Thomas Browne's skull would have had a pair of eye-sockets either side of, and just above, the nasal cavity. Furthermore, the individual bones comprising the rabbit's skull would all have had their counterparts in Sir Thomas Browne, and would have fitted together in the same order. But why stop at just the skull, and why limit ourselves to a rabbit and Sir Thomas Browne? Amphibians, reptiles, birds, mammals, we all have the same basic body-plan: a head at one end, a tail at the other, four limbs with digits on their extremities, composite bone skulls housing brains and eyes and other sense organs. Even fish are broadly the same, albeit with fins instead of proper limbs.

Just three years after Robert Fitch finished poking around with Sir Thomas Browne's skull (without, as far as I'm aware, actually comparing it with a rabbit's), the great British anatomist Richard Owen defined the word *homologue* (nowadays, most biologists would say *homology*) to mean "the same organ in different animals under every variety of form and function". The variety of form and function bit is important: 'organs' don't need to look the same, or even to have the same use, to be homologies. The arm and hand of a human, the wing of a bat or bird, the front flipper of a whale, the front leg and claw of a lizard, the front leg and hoof of a horse or sheep, the front leg and paw of a rabbit or dog, are all *homologous*: they are all forelimbs containing a humerus (in humans, the upper-arm bone), radius and ulna (the lower-arm bones), carpals (wrist bones), metacarpals (hand bones), and phalanges (finger bones—*Now, hear the word of the Lord!*). The fact that, superficially, a human hand looks nothing like a bat's wing, or a sheep's cloven hoof, and has entirely different uses, doesn't detract from the fact that, beneath the skin, the same bones are all there, albeit in widely different shapes and proportions.

Although he was by no means the first anatomist to recognise homologies between species—an observation which could be said to go back as far as Aristotle—Owen spent a large part of his professional career studying them. In 1849, he gave a discourse at the Royal Institution entitled *On the Nature of Limbs*, in which he discussed the homologous nature of vertebrate skeletons, with particular reference to their limbs. Owen was convinced that *all* vertebrate skeletons are homologous, and went on to describe a basic, generic, divinely inspired 'blueprint' for them. He referred to this blueprint as the *archetype*. In the monograph documenting his Royal Institution talk, he wrote:

> [T]*he knowledge of such a being as Man must have existed before Man appeared. For the Divine mind which planned the Archetype also foreknew all its modifications.*

Owen effectively saw his *archetype* as the Platonic 'ideal form' of vertebrate, conceived in the mind of God. God based the design of all vertebrates, including Man, on this overarching theme.

Charles Darwin first met Richard Owen in October 1856, less than a month after Darwin's return to Britain following his voyage around the world aboard *H.M.S. Beagle*. They met at a dinner party arranged by the great geologist Charles Lyell, whose books had inspired Darwin during the voyage. A short time later, Darwin managed to persuade Owen to take responsibility for describing some of the fossil skeletons he had collected on the voyage. Owen, the up-and-coming Hunterian Professor at the Royal College of Surgeons, proved to be a useful contact for Darwin, who was now trying to develop his own scientific career. But the two men never became close friends. In later years, they effectively became enemies, albeit not openly hostile ones: Victorian decorum needed to be maintained.

When Darwin eventually came to develop his theory of evolution by means of Natural Selection, he realised that Owen's homology work could provide useful support. In the margin of his copy of Owen's *On the Nature of Limbs*, he noted:

> *I look at Owen's Archetypes as more than ideal, as a real representation as far as the most consummate skill and loftiest generalizations can represent the parent form of the Vertebrata.*

Darwin had realised that Owen's *archetype* reflected not a common blueprint, but a common ancestor. Modern-day vertebrates' skeletons are analogous because they all inherited their underlying shapes, with strikingly different evolutionary modifications, from their common ancestor. Which makes a lot more sense, when you think about it. Why on earth would an omnipotent, intelligent creator feel compelled to restrict Themself to a generic design when knocking together the vertebrates? Especially when some generic features make no sense at all in certain creatures. Why, for example, would God give certain whales rear leg bones and a pelvis, buried deep within their flesh, totally detached from the rest of the whales' skeletons? Other than wanting them to *move in mysterious ways*, I mean. I'm sure creationists will have some specious answer—they always do—but the true explanation for these bones is that whales are descended from ancestors that used to walk on dry land. Their useless pelvises and leg bones are diminished, vestigial organs that have hung around, for the time-being at least, because they weren't doing the whales too much harm. Indeed, one recent scientific study indicates that certain whales' vestigial pelvises have been co-opted to allow the males to support and control longer penises. But this is a bodged re-adaptation of an outdated organ. What sort of all-powerful, intelligent designer Who took any pride in Their work would come up with a messy kludge like that? They would have the luxury of doing the job properly. But, unlike any hypothetical, omnipotent, omniscient creator, evolution has constraints. It is constrained by history. Evolution can only proceed by tweaking what has worked previously, or re-purposing what is already there. Our evolutionary history is recorded in the imperfect, inelegant designs of our bodies.

When, after twenty years' research, Darwin finally wrote his masterpiece, *On the Origin of Species*, he made several, approving references to Owen's work. But, in summing up the arguments for and against his theory, he made one major *faux pas*, stating:

The several difficulties [concerning the theory] *here discussed* [...] *are all undoubtedly of the gravest nature. We see this in the plainest manner by the fact that all the most eminent palæontologists, namely Cuvier, Owen, Agassiz, Barrande, Falconer, E. Forbes, &c., and all our greatest geologists, as Lyell, Murchison, Sedgwick, &c., have unanimously, often vehemently, maintained the immutability of species.*

Owen was incensed to be listed amongst those who claimed that species can never change. In fairness to Darwin, Owen's views on the subject of evolution were far from clear, and themselves evolved over time. He seems to have believed that species had indeed evolved, but were pre-ordained to evolve in a particular way, within certain constraints set by God. Owen's *archetype* was, he believed, one such constraint. In a scathing, anonymous review of *Origin*, Owen, writing about himself in the third person, stated:

In his last published work Professor Owen does not hesitate to state 'that perhaps the most important and significant result of palæontological research has been the establishment of the axiom of the continuous operation of the ordained becoming of living things'. The italics are the author's. As to his own opinions regarding the nature or mode of that 'continuous creative operation', the Professor is silent.

Owen goes on to claim that:

We have searched in vain, from Demaillet to Darwin, for the evidence or the proof, that it is only necessary for one individual to vary, be it ever so little, in order to [support] *the conclusion that the variability is progressive and unlimited, so as, in the course of generations, to change the species, the genus, the order, or the class. We have no objection to this result of 'natural selection' in the abstract; but we desire to have reason for our faith. What we do object to is, that science should be compromised through the assumption of its true character by mere hypotheses, the logical consequences of which are of such deep importance.*

Ouch! Owen is saying that Darwin has failed to make a sufficiently compelling case for evolution by means of Natural Selection. But the tone of this and his subsequent writings makes it clear that he would never be convinced. Although Owen was undoubtedly a brilliant anatomist and palaeontologist, his scientific views were—as was evolution, according to those views—constrained within certain limits that could not be breached. However the organic world might evolve over time, Owen knew that a pre-ordaining God would have to be involved somewhere.

But, even taking into account such religious, philosophical constraints, Owen knew that his own evolutionary views, were he ever to express them clearly, would still be seen as controversial. The British scientific establishment at the time was deeply conservative and Anglican. A relentlessly ambitious and astute political figure, Owen knew not to rock the boat by hypothesising on the nature of organic change. This goes a long way to explaining why his views on evolution came across as unclear and inconsistent. Owen's *kowtowing* to the scientific establishment, however, set him on a collision course with up-and-coming *Young Turks* intent on reform. Young Turks such as Darwin's friend Thomas Henry Huxley.

Unlike Darwin, Huxley showed little reticence in launching open attacks on Owen. There was almost certainly an element of picking a fight with a major player to establish a name for himself in Huxley's animosity towards the great anatomist. But the animosity was also genuine: Owen seemed to stand for everything Huxley stood against. So, when Owen launched a campaign to have the natural history collections of the British Museum relocated to their own purpose-built museum in South Kensington, Huxley naturally opposed the move. It was quite clear who would be put in charge of such a museum. Even Darwin opposed the plans initially. But Owen eventually won the day, and was indeed appointed as the first Superintendent of what would eventually become known as London's *Natural History Museum*.

Far more interesting than political arguments about museums, however, were Huxley and Owen's scientific clashes—particularly those on the subject of Darwinian theory. Initially opposed to the very idea of the transmutation of species, Huxley had been courted by Darwin prior to the publication of *Origin*, as somebody who needed to be won over to the cause. In an essay entitled *On the Reception of the 'Origin of Species'*, written almost three decades after the event, Huxley reflected:

> *The 'Origin' provided us with the working hypothesis we sought. Moreover, it did the immense service of freeing us for ever from the dilemma—refuse to accept the creation hypothesis, and what have you to propose that can be accepted by any cautious reasoner? In 1857, I had no answer ready, and I do not think that any one else had. A year later, we reproached ourselves with dullness for being perplexed by such an inquiry. My reflection, when I first made myself master of the central idea of the 'Origin', was, "How extremely stupid not to have thought of that!"*

Huxley wasted no time in becoming Darwin's most vociferous supporter, earning himself the nickname *Darwin's Bulldog*. The day after the publication of *On the Origin of Species*, he wrote to Darwin in Ilkley to express his admiration for the book, stating:

> *I trust you will not allow yourself to be in any way disgusted or annoyed by the considerable abuse and misrepresentation which, unless I greatly mistake, is in store for you. Depend upon it you have earned the lasting gratitude of all thoughtful men. And as to the curs which will bark and yelp, you must recollect that some of your friends, at any rate, are endowed with an amount of combativeness which (though you have often and justly rebuked it) may stand you in good stead.*
>
> *I am sharpening up my claws and beak in readiness.*

Owen was, without doubt, one of the *curs* that Huxley had in mind as he sharpened his claws. Owen's initial response to *Origin*, prior to his anonymous review, was as confusing as his views on evolution. In a letter written to Lyell a few weeks after *Origin* came out, Darwin described a meeting with Owen:

> *Under garb of great civility, he was inclined to be most bitter & sneering against me. Yet I infer from several expressions, that at bottom he goes immense way with us.— He was quite savage & crimson at my having put his name with defenders of immutability. When I said that was my impression & that of others, for several had remarked to me, that he would be dead against me: he then spoke of his own position in science & that of all the naturalists in London, "with your Huxleys", with a degree of arrogance I never saw approached. He said to effect that my explanation was best ever published of manner of formation of species. I said I was very glad to hear it. He took me up short, "you must not at all suppose that I agree with in all respects". […] We parted with high terms of consideration; which on reflexion I am almost sorry for.— He is the most astounding creature I ever encountered.*

The publication of *On the Origin of Species* created quite a stir in the popular press. Darwin had deliberately steered clear of discussing the evolution of humans, famously limiting himself to predicting, in one of the greatest understatements in the history of science, that "Light will be thrown on the origin of man and his history". The implications of his theory on Man's formerly exalted position in Nature were, however, clear for all to see. Suddenly, comparisons between humans and apes became all the rage. Darwin's critics naturally expected Owen to support their position that humans were quite distinct from apes. Darwin's disciples expected a fight. Ever since his early Hunterian career, Owen had studied the comparative anatomy of apes and humans. Everywhere he looked, he saw the need to emphasise their differences. In 1844, he wrote:

> *The Chimpanzee being the highest organized quadrumanous animal and the first in the descensive scale, from Man, every difference between its anatomy and the Human exemplifies in the most instructive manner the characteristic peculiarities of the human organisation.*

By 1858, however, just a year before the publication of *Origin*, Owen had begun to acknowledge the similarities between humans and apes:

> *I cannot shut my eyes to the significance of that all-pervading similitude of structure—every tooth, every bone, strictly homologous,—which makes the determination of the difference between Homo* [man] *and Pithecus* [orang-utan] *the anatomist's difficulty.*

To keep mankind's special place in nature, Owen decided that he needed to concentrate on the feature universally acknowledged as most clearly defining humans: their unique brain. Thus began his great battle with Huxley over the similarity (or otherwise) of the brains of humans and apes.

The battle, which dragged on for a number of years, was characterised by the two great anatomists' repeatedly making subtly different comparisons between the brains of humans and members of the order *Quadrumana* (apes, monkeys, lemurs, etc.). Huxley maintained that there was far less difference between the brain of a human and the 'highest' of the *Quadrumana* (which, at the time, was believed to be the recently discovered gorilla), than between the 'highest' of the Quadrumana and the 'lowest' (the lemur). Owen, on the other hand, contended that there was far more difference between the brain of a human and the 'highest' of the *Quadrumana*, than between the 'highest' of the Quadrumana and the *next 'highest'*. These two contentions are not necessarily contradictory, but that wasn't how the public, or either of the combatants, appears to have seen it.

The high-point for Huxley came when he conclusively demonstrated that the *hippocampus minor*, a small fold at the back of the brain, which Owen had claimed was unique to humans, was also to be found in the brains of apes.

The British public relished the unseemly battle, which was celebrated in prose, play, cartoon and verse. It was even satirised in Charles Kingsley's classic 1863 children's book, *The Water Babies*:

[Professor Ptthmllnsprts] *held very strange theories about a good many things. He had even got up once at the British Association, and declared that apes had hippopotamus majors in their brains just as men have. Which was a shocking thing to say; for, if it were so, what would become of the faith, hope, and charity of immortal millions? You may think that there are other more important differences between you and an ape, such as being able to speak, and make machines, and know right from wrong, and say your prayers, and other little matters of that kind; but that is a child's fancy, my dear. [...] No, my dear little man; always remember that the one true, certain, final, and all-important difference between you and an ape is, that you have a hippopotamus major in your brain, and it has none; and that, therefore, to discover one in its brain will be a very wrong and dangerous thing, at which every one will be very much shocked, as we may suppose they were at the professor.*

Whatever the true merits of the debate, in the eyes of the British public, Huxley was perceived to have won the battle, and Owen has gone down as an archetypical villain of popular scientific history. This is far from fair. Owen certainly had many faults: he pandered to the Anglican scientific establishment, didn't take criticism at all well, seldom acknowledged his own mistakes, and didn't always give credit where credit was due. But he was one of the greatest scientific figures of the Victorian Age, continuing his brilliant career until his official retirement in his 80th year. He was also the palaeontologist who, in 1842, formally identified a "distinct tribe or sub-order of Saurian Reptiles", and gave it the indescribably wonderful name *Dinosauria*.

For many years, Owen's statue claimed pride of place on the central stairway of his greatest memorial, the Natural History Museum in London. But, in 2009, in an affront which would have turned Owen *savage & crimson* once again, his statue was moved upstairs to make way for that of another great scientist: Charles Robert Darwin. It seems only right that Darwin should take

pride of place in any natural history museum—
especially in what was his bicentennial year—but I, for
one, had misgivings. This is how things are forgotten,
how entropy wins. Owen's statue now stands in an
obscure, dimly lit corner of the museum, within spitting
distance of that of his greatest rival, Thomas Henry
Huxley.

A rabbit skull would look really cool on a bookshelf in
the study. Should I take it home? I have to say, I'm
tempted. I don't know what Jen would say. Actually,
that's bollocks, I know exactly what Jen would say: she
would simply shake her head and mutter, "More
clutter!"

But, no, these bones were made from the Moor.
Their calcium and other precious minerals were
ingested by the rabbit while it lived on the Moor. Now
it's dead, the minerals should stay on the Moor, to be reabsorbed over time into the acid peat. Entropy at work
once again. *Earth to earth, ashes to ashes, bog to bog.*

Time to go. I look ahead, down the track. Twenty
metres away, a rabbit's head pokes out of the heather. A
live rabbit's head. It has seen me through its side-
mounted eye-sockets, but remains motionless. There's a
notch in its right ear, a trophy, perhaps, from some close
escape. A rabbit that, unlike the one at my feet, lived to
see another day. I wonder if they were related. Well,
obviously they were, but I wonder how closely.

I shift slightly, and the rabbit is gone.

Wet

The first week in January. At this time of year, you expect a certain amount of bad weather. This year has already exceeded all expectations. Three days of gales: the house battered, leaking windows, soot-falls down the chimney. Our driveway has become a new tributary to the River Calder. I've been struggling heroically—albeit unproductively—on a chapter about rooks. The rain and hail hammering against the study windows have been off-putting to say the least. Well, that's my excuse. Lights on in the middle of the day; a rattling bedroom window closed at night; a bunged-up nose in the morning. I was beginning to go stir-crazy.

Then, out of nowhere, a change in the weather: blue sky and sunshine! What more excuse did I need? Half an hour later, I'm passing through the gate on to the Moor in my wellington boots. Something tells me my normal walking boots wouldn't pass muster this afternoon.

Within seconds, a grouse and I have startled each other out of our respective wits. The grouse heads off over the quarry, *guk-guking* all the way. I've never seen one so close to the edge of the Moor before. Perhaps it had come down here looking for shelter—or maybe just for dry land.

After my heart has stopped pounding, I head on through the second gate. I was right about the wellies: the sunken track is a stream. Ankle-deep running water seeps invisibly from the surrounding peat. Even without further rain, it will continue to seep like this for days. The Moor has become one huge bog; a sodden sponge whose water is slowly pushing itself out under its own weight.

I needed to get out of the house. After a week of Christmas binges, and a restless night of stale air, I needed to clear my head, to remind myself what fresh air feels like. *Fresh* is certainly the word for it: the rain might have gone, but the wind has only let up slightly. I've wrapped up well against the weather, but, in my unseemly haste to get on to the Moor, I appear to have left my gloves at home. I draw my hands into my coat-sleeves and soldier on.

Rooks! Rooks and jackdaws! About fifty of them, billowing in from the top field. They land in the lee of the hill in a squabble of *craas* and *chaks*. That's handy: I've been trying to write about rooks all morning! Watch and observe. But they soon spot me, the lone vertical figure in the flatness, and take to the air once more: a black blizzard buffeted back east.

I reach the point where the track enters the perma-bog. The water is deeper here. Clumps of moor-grass poke from pools. I can no longer make out the track, but

I know where I'm heading. I wade on.

Up at the trig point, three days of rain have doused any trace of dust from the air. The world has a lucid, *scrubbed* feel to it. If I shelter my eyes from the wind, I can see for miles. The hyper-clear air has foreshortened perspective, removing the subtle clues haze imparts of relative distances. Everything seems magnified, as if I'm looking through binoculars, but in wide-angle. The sky is deep blue, cloudless except on the horizon. A rising gibbous moon, four days from full, hangs semi-transparent in the east. There will be a frost tonight.

I turn north along the track. The wind blows into my left nostril, ensnotting the right. This should clear my sinuses. The track is a morass of quagmires and pools. I squelch and slosh through them, veering left at the first grouse-butt, and making my way across the boggier-than-usual bog.

The track widens as I head down the slope. It's too steep here for puddles: the mud has taken on extra water. My boots sink and slide deeper. To my left, a temporary spring babbles out of sight in the heather. A small rill spills down on to the track just above where it narrows again and steps down. The step has transformed into a waterfall. I splash down it, de-mudding my boots. The track is now, beyond any doubt, a stream.

Near the bottom of the slope, a second rill joins us, tumbling over another mini-waterfall into a makeshift pool. A third rill feeds into the pool from the north. It's always wet at this corner of the Moor, but I've never seen it this wet before. I stand in the pool, looking down at submerged grass. It reminds me of seaweed. To the south, the pool drains into a half-hearted, overgrown ditch running alongside the drystone wall at the edge of the Moor. I try to work out where the water will end up: cascading down the falls at Ibbot Royd and Nutclough is my best guess, before joining Hebden Water just above its confluence with the Calder; and then, who knows how much later, flowing into the Humber, and out into the North Sea. My temporary, little rill will end up crossing almost the full width of Yorkshire, west to east.

More water is seeping out of the Moor on to the path above the ditch, creating a parallel watercourse. It runs metallic in the low light. I step out of the pool and up on to the path, following it downstream alongside the wall and ditch. The stream channels between puddles and pools, creating standing wave-ridges that look for all the world like solid ice—an observation that makes me realise just how cold it has become. What little heat there was has disappeared from the sun. It must be ten minutes at most from sunset, yet there's not a hint of red in the sky, just a smudge of tobacco-stain yellow.

Pausing to look over the gate, I zip my jacket collar higher. The sheep in the field ignore me. Wheezing gulls driven inland by the gales tease a solitary crow. Casual water sparkles in the fields below, towards home. *Waterlogged*, a strange word: I get the *water*, but why - *logged*? Even the *Oxford English Dictionary* struggles for an explanation, hazarding an educated guess that it means "to reduce (a ship) to the condition of a log", that is "to render (a ship, etc.) unmanageable by flooding with water". It's one of many nautical terms adopted unwittingly by us land-lubbers: terms such as *shake a leg*, *batten down the hatches*, and, indeed, *land-lubber*. Not that I feel particularly *land-lubberish* today; more *amphibian*.

We live on a watery planet. Over 70% of the earth's surface is water. Yet it wasn't always so. According to my grossly simplistic understanding of current thinking, when the solar system formed through the accretion of gas and dust, the heavy matter with high melting points tended to coalesce nearer the sun, eventually forming the four rocky inner planets: Mercury, Venus, Earth and Mars. The lighter material could only coalesce farther out, where it was less hot, which explains why the outer planets are gaseous giants. Most of the solar system's water ended up in this cooler region. Then, during a cataclysmic period known as the *Late Heavy Bombardment*, asteroids and comets from the outer solar system pelted the rocky inner planets. These brought water to the inner solar system. Until recently, it was thought that most of Earth's water must have come from asteroid impacts. Remote spectroscopic analyses of water from comets showed that it contained significantly different proportions of isotopes from the water found on Earth. However, in 2011, Europe's *Herschel Space Telescope* analysed water from Comet Hartley 2, finding it to contain isotope ratios similar to those found on Earth. Hartley 2 differed from the comets that had previously been analysed in that it originated from a region of the solar system beyond the orbit of Neptune known as the *Kuiper Belt*. The other comets analysed were believed to have originated from much farther out in the solar system, from a hypothetical region known as the *Oort Cloud*.

Life as we know it is serendipitous. Had fewer comets or asteroids hit the young Earth, it might have no oceans, and life might never have evolved. Had more comets or asteroids hit the planet, it might have been entirely covered in ocean, meaning that, had life evolved, and had it taken roughly the same path (which is one hell of an assumption), we might all still be fish. Which we are, to some extent: *glorified fish*.

I move on, my feet squelching into and popping out of the mud: the sound of wellington boots doing their job. I visited the Duke of Wellington's house in Hampshire once. I can't say I was overly impressed. Some old dear in the ticket office chided me for wearing a sun-hat on the hottest day of the year. Sun-hats were an affront to the memory of the former Prime Minister and hero of Waterloo, it seemed. I shall make a point of wearing my wellies next time, in solemn tribute.

A rabbit scuttles from behind a grassy tussock and splashes off through the puddles, water flying in all directions. Rabbits must spend a significant proportion of their waking hours terrified out of their minds. Don't feel sorry for them, it's an effective survival strategy. As my eyes follow the creature, I spot a small speck hanging motionless in the updraught above the edge. Even at this distance, it's clearly a kestrel, hunting for small rodents, making the most of the last few minutes of daylight.

The sun has disappeared behind Stoodley Pike. Finally, a weak, midwinter-red glow appears in the sky. It really has gone cold. Time to pick up the pace and head for home.

A pin-prick first star appears in the deepening blue: *the Evening Star*. Not a star at all, but the rocky inner planet Venus, as ever, not far from our nearest true star, the sun.

I'm not the only one with thoughts of home. The kestrel banks right and speeds along the edge towards me. It shoots past, close to the moon, heading for some secret roost in the gloaming.

Rooks

Back along the drystone wall below the edge, and over the stile. I don't often come this way, but today I felt like a change.

A trio of rooks appears over the hill as I approach the ruined building at *Johnny House* just below the quarry. They bob and weave in the hill's blustery updraught, *craaing* and *hrocing* wantonly, unconcerned by my presence. Anyone who says that animals can't experience emotions has never witnessed the unrestrained joy of rooks cavorting in the wind for the sheer hell of it.

When we think of avian aeronautics, we think of the likes of peregrines, swifts, and albatrosses: creatures whose aerial expertise can't be denied. We tend not to think of rooks. But what rooks lack in speed or endurance, they more than make up for with their ability to read and exploit the wind. They are masters of the buffet and squall, soaring and tumbling at will, while lesser fliers take shelter and wait for the wind to subside. Rooks might hunt for food in the earth, but air is their true element.

The three rooks split and loop, barrel and yo-yo. Apparently chaotic at first, patterns begin to emerge. The birds' manoeuvres are determined by mysterious rules of engagement. There is strategy involved, strategy and tactics: *rook takes rook takes rook*. What on earth is going through their minds as they barnstorm?

One of the birds breaks away and heads off towards the fields below. Two remain. We enter the middle-game. A new pattern emerges. The idea seems to be to try to position yourself behind your opponent, like an attacking aircraft in a dogfight. The lead bird soars upwards about ten metres, trading ground-speed for altitude, forcing its opponent—or, more likely, its mate—to pass underneath. It then drops back down, its mate's tail now clearly in its sights. But its mate—the new lead bird—isn't to be outwitted: it copies the manoeuvre, taking up its place once more behind the original lead bird. They're playing a strange version of *follow-my-leader* where both players seem to think the other should be in the lead. Over and over again, the birds repeat the manoeuvre, an elegant vertical waltz with occasional improvisations and flourishes.

I could watch rooks for hours. I *have* watched rooks for hours. They're one of my favourite birds, one of Britain's eight species of crow: magpie, jay, carrion crow, hooded crow, chough, jackdaw, raven, and rook. I say eight species, but the count fluctuates, the hooded crow sometimes being classified as a sub-species of the carrion crow, and sometimes as a separate species in its own right. At the moment, I'm pleased to report, the common-sense of the species-splitters seems to hold sway.

Corvids is how we're supposed to refer to the crow family, from the Latin *corvus*, meaning *crow*. It can get confusing: when some people (including me) say *crow*, they mean *member of the crow family*; when others say *crow*, they mean *carrion crow*. When I mean *carrion crow*, I say *carrion crow*.

The carrion crow and rook are the most difficult of the eight British species to tell apart: they're both black, similar in size, and crow-shaped. Physically, there isn't much else to go on. Even from good photographs, I've sometimes struggled to tell one from the other. Mature adult rooks are relatively easy to spot, in the right light at least, thanks to the characteristic pale, bare patches around the bases of their beaks. From a distance, these patches look like bone, making the birds' beaks seem bigger than they really are. In reality, the bare patches are neither beak nor bone, but featherless skin. But juvenile rooks have no such bare patches, so are difficult to distinguish from carrion crows. One marker to look out for is the skirt of loose feathers around the rook's upper legs, commonly referred to as *baggy trousers* or *pantaloons*. Then there's the purplish sheen of the rook's feathers; the carrion crow is a duller, matt black. But by far the easiest way to tell rooks from carrion crows is to count them: if you see a lot of birds together, it's a safe bet you're looking at rooks—most likely accompanied by their smaller cousins, jackdaws. Rooks and jackdaws are sociable creatures; carrion crows are real loners, usually only hanging out in breeding pairs.

But this lone pair of crows are clearly a couple of rooks: their bare, grey face-patches catch the light as they whirl, *craa* and whoop above the not-quite-dead tree. Well, perhaps not quite *whoop*.

It's unusual to see a single pair of rooks like this. Around here, they tend to congregate in groups of twenty of more, walking the fields, or weaving above them. Watching a decent-sized flock of rooks and jackdaws flying above the fields on a windy day is like watching the wind itself. You suddenly become aware of the three-dimensional nature of the gusts. The birds go where the wind takes them, shooting up and down, in and out, scattering and gathering back. There's no way you can keep track of the individual trajectories; you simply have to stand back and admire the intricate choreography.

One strange, quite possibly imagined phenomenon I've noticed concerning rooks is that they seem to fly in pairs within the flock. This, in itself, might not be all that surprising: many species of crow, including rooks, are believed to mate for life. But I've pretty much convinced myself that each pair of rooks within a flock tends to keep its wing-beats synchronised. Not only do the birds in each pair fly closely together, but they flap their wings in unison. I can't remember when I first noticed this, but once I had, I kept on noticing it. I've even studied photographs I took especially for the purpose, and swear blind I can pair the birds off from the position of their wings alone. If anyone else were to make such a claim, I'd call it bullshit. So no offence taken, call me bonkers, but check it out for yourself, and be prepared, as the Americans say, to *eat crow*.

Those crazy Yanks! Don't they know that eating crow is forbidden? Aren't they familiar with *Leviticus* 11:13–15?

> *And these ye shall have in abomination among the fowls; they shall not be eaten, they are an abomination: the eagle, and the ossifrage, and the ospray, And the vulture, and the kite after his kind; Every raven after his kind;*

The Good Lord Himself commandeth that crows should be kept off the menu. Not that they ever were. It turns out that, far from being an abomination, rooks are pretty tasty. They're pleasantly gamey, by all accounts. A bit like rabbit. In his diary entry for 20th January 1775, Gilbert White recorded an unforeseen benefit of one extraordinarily cold spell of weather:

> *Mr Hool's man says that he caught this day in a lane near Hackwood-park, many rooks, which attempting to fly fell from the trees with their wings frozen together by the sleet, that froze as it fell. There were, he affirms, many dozens so disabled! It is certain that Mr H's man did bring home many rooks & give them to the poor neighbours.*

Mr Hool's man didn't give the rooks to his neighbours as pets; they were intended for the pot.

In his *Notes and Letters on the Natural History of Norfolk*,

Sir Thomas Browne also mentions the nutritional value of rooks, their livers', unbeknownst to Browne, being a cheap and readily available source of vitamin D:

Rookes which by reason of the great quantitie of corn feilds & Rooke groues are in great plentie the yong ones are commonly eaten sometimes sold in Norwich market and many are killd for their Liuers in order to cure of the Rickets.

It turns out we all learnt about the tastiness of rooks when we were children, even though we might not have realised it:

Sing a song of sixpence,
  A pocket full of rye.
Four and twenty black birds,
  Baked in a pie.

Black birds, not *blackbirds*: the birds baked in the pie were rooks. Well, probably. You needed so many of them because there's not much meat on a rook. Six pence for a pie crammed with the meat of twenty-four rooks: a bargain by anyone's reckoning!

Rook pie is still on the menu in some rural pubs, although the authorities are beginning to clamp down on the delicacy. It's still legal to eat rooks, provided they've been shot under licence, but it's illegal to sell their meat. New gastronomic rules brought in under the 1981 *Wildlife and Countryside Act* to protect endangered birds also protect the rook.

The sound of rooks *craaing* noisily above the fields, or

in their communal rookeries and roosts, is the sound of the British countryside. Wherever there's farmland, save for in the far north of Scotland, you can hear their boisterous, echoing calls. It's a paradoxical sound: harsh, yet somehow mellow. It's also a profoundly nostalgic and comforting sound. The sound of the woods and field edges of my native Wirral. More recently, it's also become the sound of my Yorkshire home—especially at twilight, when, in the words of Macbeth:

Light thickens,
And the Crow makes Wing toth' Rookie Wood…

The first-century BCE poet Virgil was also familiar with the sight and sound of rooks heading home *en masse* after a long day in the fields:

…a host
Of rooks from food returning in long line
Clamour with jostling wings.

Many an evening, I've stood in our garden, watching the rooks heading off to their roosts in Old Town, and westward across the valley to who knows where. The air is filled with their hoarse calls. It is a wonderful sound: not so much the clichéd *caw*, as a more raucous *craa!* The Anglo-Saxons had another of their calls right, giving the bird the onomatopoeic name *hróc*, which was later corrupted into the less onomatopoeic *rook*. The name, incidentally, has nothing to do with the chess piece.

When Carl Linnaeus came to give the rook its official

scientific name, he plumped for *Corvus frugilegus*: *the grain-gathering crow*. His contemporary, the eighteenth-century author, poet and physician Oliver Goldsmith, who was evidently something of a rook fan, objected to this epithet in his multi-volume work, *A History of the Earth and Animated Nature*, stating in a footnote:

> *The husbandman, or farmer, is often unconscious of the good these industrious birds do for him at all seasons, except only in long-continued drought, when the insects descend into the earth, and when its surface becomes so hard as to defy the efforts of the rooks to dig the larvæ out. At such times, indeed, when their natural instincts are neutralized, and when hunger craves, they will in troops fall upon a field of wheat or barley just ripening, and where they will do considerable damage if not scared-off by a sentinel with a racket, or by hanging rags, dipped in melted brimstone, on sticks about the field. But the farmer is unwilling, for their thievish crime, to agree that they are otherwise serviceable to him, because he can see where rooks have been at work; single plants of wheat or grass actually pulled out of the ground, which to him appears another unpardonable offence. But if he would examine such depredations closely, he would find that the bird had only pulled up a sickly plant, to reach the grub that was feeding on its roots, and which, but for the rook, would have disrooted many more. [...] And as the question concerning the good or bad properties of the rook to the farmers is very differently believed, let any one who has doubts shoot, or have one shot for him, when the bird is on his way home from the feeding ground. Let him open the provision pouch and look at the contents; this he will find consists entirely of the larvæ of insects, which are bred and fed on the roots of plants in the ground. In this great and good service the rook is assisted by the*

214

jackdaw and starling, which are almost always seen associated on places where grubs abound.

Goldsmith overstates his case for the defence. Anyone might think that barley wouldn't crack in a rook's beak. But he's correct in identifying subterranean invertebrates as the bird's chief source of food, and in stating that rooks can be of benefit to farmers. None of which has saved the rook from persecution over the years. Their similarity to carrion crows is much to blame, the rook taking the rap for the offences of the crow. When she finds the eyes of her new-born lambs pecked, my friend the farmer isn't particularly interested in whether the culprits were rooks, carrion crows, or jackdaws; they're all just 'crows' to her.

The culprits of the lamb-peckings are almost certainly carrion crows. But misidentification and travesties of justice can work two ways. When farmers plant human simulacra in fields to protect their crops, they call them *scarecrows*. No self-respecting carrion crow would be caught dead eating crops; the deterrents should rightly be called *scare-rooks*.

Rook persecution has gone on for centuries, but the rot really set in with Henry VIII. In his *Preservation of Grain Act* of 1532, 'Old Coppernose' published an official list of 'vermin' whose persecution was mandated by law. Rewards were offered for the heads of all manner of creatures, including the:

innumerable nombre of Rookes Crowes and Choughes [which] *do daily brede and increase throughout this Realme, which Rookes Crowes and Choughes do yerely destroye devoure and consume a wonderfull and marvelous great quantitie of Corne and Greyne of all kyndes.*

Rooks aren't the only crows maligned through misidentification, it would seem. King Hal's condemnation of *choughs* is another case of mistaken identity. He clearly means *jackdaws*. The jackdaw-sized chough is found on coastal cliff-tops, not in cornfields. Fortunately for the rook, however, many farmers seem to have realised, like Goldsmith, that the birds could also be beneficial in pest-control, so turned a deaf ear to royal decree. But other wildlife was persecuted mercilessly, with some species, such as the red kite and raven, still not having fully recovered.

Confession time: I'm also guilty of having blamed rooks for crimes they probably didn't commit. Every spring, to my delight, one or two pairs of lapwings return to the fields behind our house. I love to watch them tumbling and swooping in their spectacular courtship displays. A few weeks later, their flights turn defensive. They flap back and forth in a frantic state, fending off scores of rooks and jackdaws from their nests. The odds seem stacked against them. How can the poor lapwings hope to raise broods with all those murderous rooks about? Lapwing populations have declined steeply in recent years. Might not this decline be due to increased numbers of the rooks, which are seldom culled these days, thanks to laudable clamp-downs on shotgun ownership? Or so I hypothesised.

Unlike me, the *Royal Society for the Protection of Birds* has looked into the matter in detail, blaming the decline in lapwing numbers primarily on changes in farming practices. I don't think reduced culling of rooks was one of the changes in farming practices they had in mind. The RSPB is more concerned about land-drainage, intensification of farming, the use of pesticides, and changes in crop-rotation. To be honest, I would expect the RSPB to hold the rook blameless—the RSPB is, after all, a bird-protection charity—but I suspect it's right. Slap on the wrists, Richard! Hypothesising with little or no evidence! Blaming rooks, like every other bugger!

I love to watch rooks feeding. They're so *laid-back*, walking the fields for hours, probing the soil with their stiletto beaks. Their beak-down, stiff-legged, baggy-pantalooned walk gives the birds an undeniably comical appearance, but they are methodical, and seem to have few problems finding enough invertebrates to eat. Leatherjackets are their favourites, apparently: the subterranean larvae of craneflies.

When they're in the fields dibbing for invertebrates, rooks spend a lot of time with their faces in the mud. It has been suggested that the adult birds' bare faces must be linked in some way with this mode of feeding. But the question is—or was—is the rook's bare face a *consequence of* digging in the mud (that is, the result of *wear and tear*), or is it an *adaptation for* digging in the mud? In other words, do mature rooks' faces naturally moult to prevent their becoming plastered in mud when they feed? Oliver Goldsmith favoured the *wear and tear* explanation, stating that the bill of the rook:

> *which, by being frequently thrust into the ground to fetch out grubs and earth-worms, is bare of feathers as far as the eyes, and appears of a whitish colour.*

Wear and tear it is, then. But not so, says Henry Forbes Witherby, author of the highly respected *Handbook of British Birds*. In a 1963 paper entitled *The Sequence of Plumages of the Rook, With Special Reference to the Moult of the "Face"*, which appeared in the ornithological journal *British Birds* (of which he was the founding editor), Witherby writes:

> *It has always been a disputed point as to whether the Rook (Corvus f. frugilegus) gets its bare "face" by means of abrasion of the feathers or by a moult. Most ornithologists have favoured the moult theory or have regarded it as a "natural peculiarity." This conclusion has been reached, however, by inference rather than actual experiment. A few somewhat trivial experiments have been made with captive birds, but no proper investigation of the subject has hitherto been undertaken so far as I am aware.*

Witherby goes on to describe a number of previous studies of rook's bald patches, all of which were unsatisfactory in one way or another. He then describes his own recent research, which avoided the pitfalls earlier investigations had fallen into studying captive birds by only studying wild rooks—83 dead rooks, to be precise, helpfully provided by an assortment of gamekeepers. The specimens were "obtained in every month and in nearly every week of the year", allowing Witherby to study rooks at all stages of their lifecycle. He used a microscope to make detailed observations of the birds' feathers throughout their moulting sequence. At one point in the paper, Witherby argues that the delicate new facial feathers which appear during the rook's moult from juvenile to first winter plumage would surely be subject to the same abrasive forces as those which supposedly wear away the facial feathers of older birds. But Witherby's microscope showed that these new feathers survive intact, indicating that abrasion is not to blame for the bare patches. He continues:

The Rook remains with its "face" fully feathered until [its second] *January, and in some individuals until a month or two later. A very gradual moult then commences on the chin, the feathers dropping out generally first in the centre of the part which afterwards becomes bare.*

Case closed: the rook's bare patch is the result of moulting, not abrasion. But why does it only happen in mature birds? If it truly were a useful adaptation associated with feeding in the soil, why would the juvenile birds not also have evolved a bare patch? Maybe it's just an evolutionary constraint: something in the rook's development cycle prevents it from losing its facial feathers earlier. Or maybe the rook's bare patch isn't an adaptation for feeding after all. In a footnote, Witherby observes:

> *I have carefully examined the generative organs of all the specimens in first summer-plumage (i.e. one year or a little more old) and have not found any in a breeding condition.*

In other words, the rook's bare patch only appears in sexually mature birds. Perhaps that might be the evolutionary constraint I'm looking for. Perhaps the loss of feathers is linked to sexual maturity—that is, to adult sex hormones. In the same way that many human males become bald after reaching sexual maturity, perhaps rooks require adult hormones to develop their bald patches. In which case, the bald patch might indeed be a useful adaptation to help with feeding in the soil, but one which is restricted by biological constraints to adult birds. Or perhaps it's not an adaptation for feeding after all. If bald patches are associated with sexual maturity, perhaps they're no more than signals to members of the opposite sex that the birds are sexually mature. *Perhaps, perhaps, perhaps.*

Here I go again, conjuring up *evolutionary Just-So stories*. It's easy, and great fun, to hypothesise, but hypotheses need to be tested. Testing hypotheses is where the hard work begins. I was really taken with Witherby's paper. It's one example amongst thousands of the noble British tradition of amateur science. *Citizen science*, they like to call it these days, but I prefer the word *amateur* (in its original, non-derogatory sense). There are still useful contributions to be made to our scientific knowledge by dedicated and gifted amateurs. Amateurs such as Henry Forbes Witherby and Charles Robert Darwin.

When they're not hunting for buried invertebrates, most of the rooks around here seem to be trying to get at the nuts and seeds in my garden bird-feeders. I've tried countermeasures, of course—a caged bird-table, designed to bar access to large birds, and modified feeders, requiring greater acrobatic skill to feed from— but the rooks always manage to circumvent them eventually. A glass feeder with no footholds has them temporarily stumped, but it's only a matter of time.

Rooks and other crows are phenomenally intelligent for animals with 'bird-brains'. They watch and learn and work things out. The fortuitously named Christopher Bird of Cambridge University has videoed captive rooks making and using tools. In one video, a rook presented with a morsel of food in a small basket at the bottom of a transparent tube takes the straight piece of wire provided, places it into the tube, and, using the tube for purchase, bends the top of the wire into a hook. The rook then removes the wire from the tube, turns it around, and re-inserts it into the tube, using the hook to retrieve the basket. A few decades ago, we arrogantly believed that *Homo sapiens* was the only species on the planet with sufficient mental capacity to devise and use tools. The chimps eventually put us straight on that front. Now, even the birds are at it!

As members of an undeniably intelligent species, we like to think that 'intelligence', however we define the word, is a particularly important trait. Because we've become increasingly intelligent during our recent evolutionary past, it's tempting to think that intelligence is somehow associated with *evolutionary advancement*. Advancement is a meaningless concept as far as evolution is concerned. Natural Selection can only work in the here and now; it can't look ahead towards some ultimate future design, so there's nothing for evolution to be advancing *towards*. But that didn't prevent some scientists from seeing intelligence as a sign of evolutionary advancement—in *all* animal species, not just our own. Using this flawed logic, many people once classified birds according to their perceived intelligence, believing it to reflect their evolutionary advancement. This explains why the crow family appeared at the very front of my first ever bird book, *The Observer's Book of Birds*, with those dimwit grouse sitting in the dunces' corner at the back (I told you they were stupid!). It was also this kind of thinking that placed penguins low down on a mythological 'evolutionary ladder' of birds, thereby justifying sending Edward A. Wilson and his colleagues on a wild penguin-egg chase in Antarctica.

Bandit at three o'clock! The two rooks peel out of their looping manoeuvres and into a genuine dogfight. A female kestrel has appeared in their airspace. This is intolerable!

The kestrel is after voles. I often see them hunting

here above the edge. Rooks aren't the only birds to make use of updraughts. But, before the kestrel can begin to hover, the rooks are on to her, *craaing* like things possessed, alerting their colleagues in the fields below. The rooks bank and combat-spread, approaching the kestrel from behind. She breaks, and they overshoot, half-heartedly pecking in her direction. Their tactic is harassment, not physical contact. They swerve right and left, bearing back round on their foe. The kestrel doesn't want any hassle. She tries to retreat in a dignified manner, but the rooks are having none of it. They shoot in close from either site, stabbing and squawking.

Mobbing, this attack behaviour is called. Many birds do it, but crows seem to relish it. Any large bird, or any bird of prey irrespective of its size, is fair game: herons, buzzards, peregrines, kestrels. It's a technique both learnt and evolved. There are obvious advantages in ganging up against predators, warning your fellow rooks of the danger, and summoning their help. But the rules of engagement are crude to say the least: herons, buzzards and kestrels are no threat to rooks. Mobbing behaviour developed to deal with genuine threats such as peregrines and goshawks. The kestrel is being mobbed because of her superficial resemblance to more dangerous raptors. It's another case of mistaken avian identity. Rooks, it turns out, are just as guilty as the rest of us at persecuting innocent birds.

The kestrel has had enough. She turns tail and flees over the hill before re-enforcements arrive. The rooks *craa* triumphantly and turn back into the wind to perform joyous victory rolls.

Ice

The BBC weather forecaster was feeling rather pleased with himself yesterday morning. Much of the European mainland has been experiencing a continental cold snap, which has dragged on for weeks. A huge high pressure zone has anchored itself over central Europe, drawing bitterly cold winds from Russia. Temperatures have dropped towards -40°C in some places. Dozens of people have died. But, until yesterday, Britain had remained unaffected.

It's been touch-and-go the last few days. The cold weather moving in from the south and east has been on a collision course with wetter, warmer weather heading in from the Atlantic. To his credit, a couple of days ago, one of the TV weather forecasters declared it too close to call, and ended up giving two totally different forecasts, depending on whether the continental or Atlantic system won the day. As it turned out, the cold prevailed. Much of England has been covered in snow. More to the point, much of South East England has been covered in snow, which made it newsworthy. It's a common observation in the North that, as far as national news is concerned, it never snows unless it snows in London.

We got off lightly for once: West Yorkshire has escaped all but lightest smattering of snow, most of which quickly blew away. But it's lung-stingingly cold—by far the coldest spell of the winter so far. Yesterday, driving north from Todmorden, I saw an entire river frozen over. There might not be any snow worth writing home about, but there's plenty of ice, including one rare and difficult-to-forecast form of ice, which yesterday's weather forecaster couldn't help remarking upon, having actually forecast it the day before: ice caused by freezing rain.

As the weather forecaster explained, freezing rain can occur when a warm front, such as the one approaching us from the Atlantic, is forced up and over a layer of much colder air, like the one just arrived from Europe. Any snow falling down into the warm zone melts into rain, but, as this rain falls down further into the much colder zone near the ground, it doesn't re-freeze, but remains supercooled. When it hits the ground, however, it instantly freezes, covering whatever it happens to strike in a thin layer of ice, known as glaze.

Yesterday morning, having gone into the garden to feed the birds, I gaped in wonder at the sight of our miniature red maple encased in a 2 mm coating of clear ice. Every twig, every nascent leaf-bud, had been sheathed to exactly the same depth, as if the whole tree had been varnished. It was then that I knew I simply had to get up on to the Moor.

Obsidian, that's the word that's been on the tip of my tongue for the last ten minutes: dark, volcanic glass. Yes, the ice-covered drystone wall at the foot of the Moor looks uncannily like obsidian, shining black-smooth in the weak sunlight. The dark millstone is no longer gritty, but polished. Only the upper surfaces have been glazed, though, as if someone poured thick, dark treacle over them. I can see how the coating flowed and spread, oozing down into gaps, dripping on to the rocks below. Some drips have frozen mid-fall, forming small icicles.

On closer inspection, I realise the coating isn't black at all; it's pure, clear ice. The dark colour comes from the weathered rocks encased beneath. The glaze would be called *black ice*, were it on the road, but, again, it would be the road surface that was black, not the ice. *Verglas*, mountain climbers call it, from the French for *glass-ice*: treacherous stuff!

I arrive at the Moor gate and try to pull it open. Exposed by my fingerless gloves, my fingertips can't get a grip. The French are right, it's just like glass. It's also unbelievably cold. I'd better be careful. I make my hands into fists and breathe deeply into them to return some body heat to my fingers. Then I wrap my right arm around the top bar of the gate and give it a good yank. It's frozen solid. I yank again, putting my full weight into it this time. The gate resists, then suddenly yields. I nearly topple over. Icicles fall from the gate, splintering on the frozen ground.

I'm reminded of the rooks that, according to Gilbert White, Mr Hool's man caught on that icy winter's day in 1775, "their wings frozen together by the sleet, that froze as it fell". Freezing rain, of course! It sounds like a tall tale, until you see what freezing rain can do.

The track up to the second gate is solid, white, and slippery, but the frozen grass-tufts give good purchase. My fingers still tingling from their encounter with the first gate, I push open the kissing-gate with my walking stick and slide through on to the Moor proper.

A tundra landscape greets me, motionless and monochrome. Spiky clusters of moor-grass stand straw-pale against dark heather. Every grass spike, every heather twiglet has been preserved in ice. Sodden-looking, yet dry and brittle.

It's colder out in the open. I zip up the collar on my

coat. Suddenly, I sense something far to my left and turn to see a large raptor—a peregrine? a short-eared owl?—launching from the heather and heading off over the rise. The long, flappy wing-beats suggest short-eared owl, but it's too far away to be sure. A long strand trails from the bird's right talon: some poor creature's innards? hay-bale twine? the leather *jess* of an escaped falconer's bird? surely not a snake! Who can tell at this distance?

The mystery bird gone, I head towards the paved track, pixie-stepping my way between frozen puddles. The track is a curling rink, too dangerous to walk on, so I crunch alongside it, over what would usually be impenetrable bog. At the foot of the steep rise, I make adjustments to my telescopic walking stick and head up the hill. Half-way to the summit, my feet start to slide backwards. I turn sideways for extra grip and continue crab-fashion. I'm glad I remembered to bring my walking stick. I don't usually bother, but, on days like today, a third leg is more than 50% more useful.

I reach the brow of the hill and look towards the trig point. *Gaa! Fell-runners!* What the hell are they doing out here on a day like today? I can barely walk, how can they possibly be running? A pair of officials in high-visibility jackets stand at the trig point doing something official-looking with clipboards as the runners pass by. I decide to give them a wide berth, even though it means I won't get to touch the trig point today.

My gaze turns east. The visibility is poor. I can only just make out the local wind power-station through the mist. Only three turbines are turning, despite there being a perfectly adequate breeze. Perhaps the freezing rain has frozen the others solid. They're the future, apparently.

On a clear day, I'd just be able to make out two massive coal-fired power stations miles to the east: Drax near Leeds, and Ferrybridge near Castleford. Like the wind turbines, these aren't energy generators, but energy converters: they convert chemical energy stored in carbon bonds within coal into heat and entropy. To save on fuel transportation costs, they were built near the local coal measures, which were laid down in swamps over 300 million years ago, when Yorkshire, and the rest of Britain, was near the equator. Although levels fluctuated, there was considerably more carbon dioxide in the atmosphere in those days, so the planet was warmer and wetter, hence the swamps. Giant lycopods and tree ferns living in the swamps photosynthesised, converting atmospheric carbon dioxide into organic compounds, some of which were buried in the swamps, eventually forming coal. This will have resulted in a decrease in the amount of carbon dioxide in the atmosphere, but a far more dramatic drop came hundreds of millions of years later, around 50 to 30 million years ago, as continents collided, throwing up huge mountain ranges, including the Himalaya and Alps. The new mountains provided newly exposed rock surfaces to be eroded. Silicate minerals in the rocks reacted with atmospheric carbon dioxide to produce bicarbonates, which were then washed into the oceans, forming new carbonate rocks. As a result, carbon dioxide levels in the atmosphere plummeted and the planet cooled, forming ice caps at the poles. For the last couple of hundred years, however, we have been digging up coal in vast quantities and burning it for fuel, thereby returning some of the long-lost carbon dioxide to the atmosphere. As a consequence, global temperatures are rising once again.

So-called *climate-change sceptics* relish days like today: if the planet's warming, how come it's so bloody cold? But such questions naively, or deliberately, confuse climate with weather.

It was the Victorian physicist John Tyndall who first measured how different gases in the atmosphere absorb heat. An Anglo-Irishman, born in 1820, he began his career working as a draughtsman for the Ordnance Survey in Ireland, eventually transferring to England. Having been dismissed by the Ordnance Survey, along with many others, for agitating for better terms and conditions, Tyndall became a railway surveyor, at one point working for the delightfully named Richard Carter of the West Riding Union Railway. He then became a teacher at a college in Hampshire before travelling to Germany to take his Ph.D., studying magnetism under the supervision of Robert Bunsen (of burner fame). Having obtained his Ph.D., Tyndall returned to Britain, where, in 1853, a new friend, Darwin's future *bulldog*, Thomas Henry Huxley, encouraged him to apply for the vacant post of Professor of Natural Philosophy at the

Royal Institution. Tyndall landed the job, working under one of the giants of nineteenth-century science, the inventor of the electric motor, Michael Faraday. He later succeeded Faraday, becoming famous, as had his predecessor, for the quality of his popular science lectures.

Both Huxley and Tyndall caught the Victorian mountaineering bug, travelling to the Alps to study glaciers and climb peaks. Tyndall managed to reach the summit of Mont Blanc, the highest peak in Western Europe, although Huxley had to give up half way. Tyndall returned to re-climb Mont Blanc several times, was a member of the first party to conquer the Weisshorn, and led the third team to conquer the Matterhorn.

Huxley and Tyndall also became close friends of Joseph Dalton Hooker and, through Hooker, Charles Darwin. In 1864, Huxley invited Tyndall and Hooker to become members of a new and exclusive scientific dining club, later dubbed *The X Club*. The club's members were friends of like mind, many of whom wished to influence British science policy. One of their key aims was to remove the Anglican religious establishment's influence on science. It was no surprise, therefore, that they were huge supporters of Darwin.

Tyndall was adamant that science should only rely on naturalistic explanations. He used the opportunity of an address to the 1874 *British Association for the Advancement of Science* to push this agenda, declaring:

All religious theories, schemes and systems, which embrace notions of cosmogony [the origin of the universe], *or which otherwise reach into the domain of science, must, in so far as they do this, submit to the control of science, and relinquish all thought of controlling it.*

Some members of the religious community were scandalised at this attempt to drive a wedge between science and religion.

In 1859—the year in which *On the Origin of Species* was published—Tyndall carried out experiments on the heat absorption properties of various gases. He assembled highly sensitive electrical apparatus which allowed him to detect the heat radiated down a long, evacuated tube from a source at the far end. Having zeroed his galvanometer, Tyndall introduced different gases into the tube, using the consequent deflection of the galvanometer to assess how much of the radiant heat the gases absorbed compared with ordinary air. He concluded that, while there were no discernible differences between the thermal absorption properties of oxygen, nitrogen, hydrogen, and ordinary air, certain other gases were far better at absorbing heat. For example, he found that carbonic oxide (the old name for carbon monoxide) was 750 times better than ordinary air at absorbing heat, and carbonic acid gas (carbon dioxide) 972 times better. The real surprise, however, came when he measured the absorption properties of water vapour. Tyndall takes up the story:

We are now fully prepared for a result which, without such preparation, might appear incredible. Water is, to some extent, a volatile body, and our atmosphere, resting as it does upon the surface of the ocean, receives from it a continual supply of aqueous vapour. [...] Compared with the great body of the air, the aqueous vapour it contains is of almost infinitesimal amount, 99.5 out of every 100 parts of the atmosphere being composed of oxygen and nitrogen. In the absence of experiment, we should never think of ascribing to this scant and varying constituent any important influence on terrestrial radiation; and yet its influence is far more potent than that of the great body of the air. To say that on a day of average humidity in England, the atmospheric vapour exerts 100 times the action of the air itself, would certainly be an understatement of the fact. Comparing a single molecule of aqueous vapour with an atom of either of the main constituents of our atmosphere, I am not prepared to say how many thousand times the action of the former exceeds that of the latter.

Much of the sunlight which hits the earth is in the visible part of the spectrum, passing through the planet's atmosphere largely unhindered—which is a good thing for those of us who rely on sunlight to see or photosynthesise. But some of that light is reflected back off the earth's surface in the invisible, infra-red part of the spectrum. Infra-red radiation is the main component of radiated heat. A proportion of this heat, as Tyndall showed, is absorbed by the water vapour in the earth's atmosphere, preventing it from being reflected back into space. Without this heat absorption, our planet would freeze. Tyndall puts it far more poetically:

A cobweb spread above a blossom is sufficient to protect it from nightly chill; and thus the aqueous vapour of our air, attenuated as it is, checks the drain of terrestrial heat, and saves the surface of our planet from the refrigeration which would assuredly accrue, were no such substance interposed between it and the voids of space.

Although he wasn't the first to suggest it, Tyndall was describing what we now call *the Greenhouse Effect*. It's an extremely good thing in moderate doses. We wouldn't be able to survive without it. The problem comes when we change the balance of gases in the atmosphere, adding more heat absorbers, such as carbon dioxide, into the mix—by burning vast amounts of coal, for example. Global temperatures rises are inevitable. To make matters worse, rising temperatures mean that the oceans heat up, releasing more heat-absorbing water vapour into the atmosphere. Warming creates water vapour, which creates more warming: a vicious cycle. Similarly, as the planet warms, huge quantities of methane—even more effective than carbon dioxide as a greenhouse gas—will be released into the atmosphere as the not-quite-*perma*-enough permafrost in the peat bogs of Alaska and Siberia begins to thaw.

It's a total mess, basically.

Perhaps it's just as well that today's poor visibility prevents me from seeing Drax power station, Britain's single largest emitter of carbon dioxide. Out of sight, out of mind. Why spoil a perfectly good walk by getting wound-up? Mind you, there are always the impotent wind turbines to irritate me. To some extent, old-fashioned religious dogma has been replaced by naive environmentalism. Tyndall was right: in matters of science, science should be left to the scientists. The sort of scientists who point out that, to reduce carbon emissions in any serious measure, we need to start building more nuclear power stations as a matter of urgency.

I turn my back on the wind turbines, with Drax invisible beyond, and head along the frozen path at the side of the quarry. The weight of the sheathing ice has bent the moor-grass over the path. I sweep at it gently with my walking stick, and it shatters. What fun! Below, grouse have seen me against the skyline, and are emitting frenzied *go-back!* calls. But, for once, they don't explode out of the heather into the air. The ice encasing the heather must make food hard to come by. In such bitterly cold conditions, the undoubted benefit of conserving energy outweighs the potential benefit of fleeing. Or maybe their wings have been frozen to their bodies by the freezing rain, like Mr Hool's man's rooks. Or perhaps they've heard there's a large, unidentified raptor in the neighbourhood. In any case, grouse are more sensible than they let on.

My thoughts return to poor John Tyndall, an overlooked hero of science. It was good (and appropriate) that a glacier, two mountains, and a centre for the study of climate change were named after him. But Tyndall is nowhere nearly as famous or celebrated today as his

friends Huxley, Hooker and Darwin. Apart from being credited with demonstrating that the Greenhouse Effect is a reality, he is mainly remembered these days for the tragic nature of his death.

Eleven years after the death of his friend Charles Darwin, the 73-year-old Tyndall was himself ailing. Bedridden, he was in the habit of taking magnesia for dyspepsia and chloral hydrate for insomnia. At the coroner's inquest, held less than a week after his death in December 1893, his widow, Louisa, explained how:

> *I was in the habit of giving* [the medication] *to him. As a rule, there were two bottles near the bed, one of magnesia and the other syrup of chloral. I was in the habit of reading the labels on the bottles and putting on one side the chloral: then I took the other one bottle. I did so on Monday. I measured a teaspoonful of magnesia, as I thought, and added water. He took this at a*

gulp, then, according to custom, a gulp of ginger. All he said was: "There is a curious sweet taste." I tasted the drop left and saw there were two bottles on the table, and found what I had taken came from the full bottle of chloral standing near, which had recently come from the chemist. [...]

I said: "John, I have given you chloral," and he said: "Yes, my poor darling, you have killed your John."

A doctor was summoned, medical almanacs were consulted, tonsils were tickled, but to no avail. It took poor John Tyndall ten hours to die from the accidental overdose administered by his darling wife.

St David's Day

The First of March. *Result!* We knocked another one off! February is, without doubt, the crappiest month of the year: Christmas long-gone, and still winter drags on! By February, it's getting beyond a joke. As my friend Mary used to say, there's a reason why they only gave it twenty-eight days. Twenty-nine, this year. I feel cheated: why can't we have leap-days in a decent month? We could have been a day further into March by now!

The First of March. *White rabbits!* Better not count my chickens, though: it nearly always snows around here some time in March, just in time for lambing season. But winter is definitely on its way out. The birds certainly think so. A robin was building a nest in the clematis outside Dad's kitchen window as I ate breakfast yesterday morning. Philip, the semi-tame pheasant that visits our garden, has attracted the attention of a brace of coy females, and has been strutting his stuff in front of them on the lawn. *Cocky* is definitely the word. Hormone-fuelled chaffinches have been chasing each other around the trees. Great tits and goldfinches have been singing their hearts out. Blue tits have been checking out the nest box in our Scots pine. And, as for the local dunnocks, the least said about what they've been up to the better.

The weather forecast predicted overcast skies, but the day dawned bright with a slight mist. By ten o'clock, the sky above the Moor was crisp and blue, with a few wispy mares' tails drifting northwards. Sod the writing! I texted my friend Bill (who insists on denying his Welsh heritage) some customary, tongue-in-cheek, St David's Day best wishes, filled my flask, pulled on my boots, and headed for the high ground.

I shouldn't have wrapped up quite so warm. The scarf was definitely not a good idea. But there was a distinct nip in the air as I left the house, and clouds of condensation billowed from my gaping mouth as I gasped my way up the hill. Up on the Moor, though, the sun has burnt away what remained of the mist. It feels noticeably warmer. Well, I suppose it would, after that climb.

Through the new kissing-gate and on to the Moor proper. Heather and sky, russet and blue. This is more like it. A few small birds are about. *Little brown jobs.* Meadow pipits, with the occasional skylark perhaps, it's hard to tell at this distance. There are no signs of grouse, they're keeping a low profile this morning. I spot a pair of rabbits fleeing through the heather fifty metres to the left—not *white rabbits*, though. Then another, bigger rabbit, scudding across the track and through the tufts of moor-grass a hundred metres ahead. No, not a rabbit, a March hare! Easy to tell from a rabbit, even at this distance: at full pelt, hares don't hop like rabbits, but gallop like horses. I'll never forget the time I nearly trod on one as I was helping bring cows down off the Moor for winter. The hare must have seen me coming, but lay low and motionless in its hollow in the ground—its *form*—hoping I'd blunder by. It didn't move, and I didn't see it, until I was less than a metre away. Then the hare lost its nerve and was off at a ridiculous pace, pursued by three hopelessly outpaced Jack Russell terriers.

Like the rabbits, my March hare isn't white, although many years ago it might have been. The native mountain hare, which turns white in winter, died out in England several thousand years ago, presumably as trees and shrubs migrated north into the hare's former territory at the end of the last glacial period. Mountain hares live on in the Scottish highlands, from where they were re-introduced to the Peak District as game in the second half of the nineteenth century. The hares we see in the rest of England, brown hares, were, it's believed, introduced by man from continental Europe in the Iron Age. According to the Roman historian Cassius Dio, Queen Boudicca used to keep a hare secreted about her person for divination purposes. I can't help feeling that tossing a coin would have been a whole lot simpler—and just as reliable.

As I turn to climb the slope, I spot a couple of rooks dibbing for invertebrates in the mud by the quarry. At this time of year, even the gregarious rook is pairing-off.

The white-faced adults, at least.

The trig point shines white, a vertical blip in the rusty heather. I make my way to it, and touch it to make it official. There's still a slight mist across the valley, but up here it's bright and clear. Cirrus clouds, cross-hatched with vapour trails, migrate across a blue, last-days-of-winter sky.

But no, not winter… Above and behind me, a melodic burbling bursts forth, announcing that spring is finally here. I turn and search the sky. It takes me a good thirty seconds to spot the minuscule dot rising high above the sun: my first skylark of the year! A skylark on St David's Day? Some mistake, surely! But there it is. And now another, a hundred metres or so to the left, and a third, far ahead.

Along with the *craaing* of the rook, the song of the skylark is the quintessential sound of the British countryside. This *blithe spirit*'s voice has been immortalised in poetry by Percy Bysshe Shelley and others, and in musical form by Charles Darwin's great-nephew Ralph Vaughan Williams. Year after year, Vaughan Williams's *The Lark Ascending* is voted Britain's favourite piece of classical music. It's undeniably wonderful—very British, very evocative, very nostalgic—although, I have to say, it's also *excruciatingly slow* if it's supposed to represent the song of a skylark. The male skylark blasts out around forty separate notes per second. In 1990, the musician and composer David Hindley slowed down 48 seconds of recorded skylark song, transcribing it into nearly thirteen minutes of sheet music. The result, played at human-speed, was said to resemble not so much Vaughan Williams as Beethoven's Fifth Symphony. If you played Vaughan Williams's masterpiece back at true skylark-speed, it would be finished in under a minute—as, indeed, would be the lead violinist.

The sound of skylarks is becoming increasingly rare these days. It's one of the sounds of my childhood. Every time I hear it, I'm back on seventh fairway at Bromborough playing golf with Dad, or standing by the caravan in Anglesey looking out to sea. Skylarks are farmland and grassland birds: you'll almost never see one in a tree. They feed exclusively on the ground, and even nest there. They were once so common that, like wheatears and other small birds, they were eaten by the wagonload. Mrs Beeton recommended stuffing nine skylarks with breadcrumbs, lemon-rind, and parsley, before baking them in a pie-dish with beef, bacon, more parsley, shallots, and stock, all topped with a layer of puff-pastry. Sounds delicious. Yet, for the last few decades, skylarks have been going through a bad patch. Changes in farming practices are thought to be to blame, as usual. Increased use of weed-killers and pesticides, combined with a move away from overwintering arable fields as stubble, means that skylarks, and many other farmland birds, simply can't find enough food to survive. To me, it sounds like an easy problem to remedy.

The skylark burbles on. The song is all about sex, of course. In addition to attracting potential mates, it most likely helps stake a territorial claim: classic Darwinian Sexual Selection in action. The male bird flies so high to ensure his song can be heard over as wide an area as possible. It might also be to show off. Any male that can fly so high while singing for so long is likely to be capable of defending his territory, and successfully fathering broods. Some male birds, like Philip the pheasant, try to attract mates with their bright plumage, but, as a general rule, the species which sing the most beautifully—skylarks, nightingales, wrens, blackcaps—tend not to need showy colours. Or, as Darwin put it in his 1871 book, *The Descent of Man, and Selection in Relation to Sex*: "with birds the power of song and brilliant colours have rarely been both acquired by males of the same species". Try telling that to a canary.

When it comes to evading would-be predators, the skylark often employs a seemingly suicidal tactic. I saw, or rather heard, it in action myself a few months back. A merlin was in hot pursuit of a skylark above a field at the edge of the Moor. The chase lasted for a good thirty seconds, although I didn't get to see the outcome. Both birds bobbed and weaved, turned and dived, the merlin never more than a metre or so behind its prey. Yet the skylark was singing for all its worth! A crazy waste of energy in a life-or-death situation. Yet it's a tactic frequently employed by skylarks. It turns out to be not so crazy after all, for the fitter birds at least. In a snappily entitled article, *Song as a pursuit-deterrent signal, and its occurrence relative to other anti-predation behaviours of skylark (Alauda arvensis) on attack by merlins (Falco columbarius),* which appeared in the journal *Behavioral Ecology and Sociobiology* in 1994, Will Cresswell explained how field observations had shown that merlins tend to give up chasing individual skylarks sooner if the skylark sings strongly. A strong song seems to act as a deterrent to merlins, which have learned—either through experience, or through Natural Selection—that strong singers also tend to be strong fliers, so are less fruitful prey. But this reasoning doesn't explain why skylarks *first* adopted the tactic, before the merlins learnt what a strong song meant. It still sounds a bit bonkers to me. But I like their attitude.

Having been singing for a good couple of minutes, the nearest skylark plunges towards the ground, maybe out of pure exhaustion, or maybe as an open invitation to would-be mates to come and check out his territory. But, if there are any takers, I can't see them.

I turn to the track and head off through the heather, still delighted at this earlier-than-expected sign of spring. And then, bang on cue, another sign: a mournful, lilting call from way across the Moor.

The curlews are back!

.

Sky

A perfect Saturday afternoon in April: blue sky, gentle breeze, warm sunshine. Spring is in full flow. I saw my first swallow of the year just over a week ago. It was swooping after flies in the tunnel of trees on Height Road, just below the Moor. It's wonderful to have them back: one swallow might not make a summer, but it does at least hold the promise that summer is finally on its way.

Flat-faced boulders jut precariously from greening bilberry in the abandoned quarry at the side of the track. The overgrown spoil heaps above me could be mistaken for ancient barrows. Behind them, the sky is just about as blue as sky can get: a bit-too-perfect, not-quite-British, Mediterranean shade of blue.

It's hard to believe that, exactly one month ago, Jen and I stood beneath genuine Mediterranean skies, sweltering in the middle of a forum in Pompeii, gazing north towards brooding Vesuvius. The last time I walked on the Moor, just before we left for Italy, there was a thin layer of ice on the reservoir above Old Town, and a few scoops of snow still lingered in the shadows of the quarries below Deer Stones Edge. Spring had seemed forever away, yet it was awaiting us on our return from Italy, just a fortnight later.

Volcanoes! Of course! That's what's wrong with the sky! Some volcano with an unpronounceable name has erupted in Iceland. As a result, all aircraft in the UK and most of northern and western Europe have been grounded. Volcanic ash in aeroplane engines could spell disaster, although nobody seems to know just how much ash it would take to bring down a plane. Governments are erring on the side of caution, which means there are no aircraft—and, therefore, no vapour trails—in this impeccable blue sky.

I'm glad that Eyjafjallajökull—for such is the Icelandic volcano's unlikely name—had the decency to wait until we were safely back in Blighty before wreaking havoc on the air-traffic system. Suddenly, Channel Tunnel notwithstanding, Great Britain feels like an island once more: if I needed to cross the Irish Sea or Atlantic right now, a boat would be my only option.

I scan the sky from horizon to horizon, just to make sure. It's as I thought: not a single vapour trail! This is quite something, situated as I am midway between Manchester and Leeds-Bradford airports. I'm surprised at just how moved I am by this unexpected turn of events. This is what springtime skies are *supposed* to look like, unmarred by that most modern of cloud formations, *Cirrus aviaticus*. Vapour trails are one of those apparently unavoidable by-products of modern technological advances that have diminished our enjoyment of the natural world, almost without our noticing. How far would you have to travel nowadays to see a night sky unadulterated by light-pollution? Or to stand in a landscape where the sound of distant cars or aircraft engines is unknown? I'm no Luddite, but it's sobering to realise just how readily we have come to accept these modern blemishes on the natural world without even questioning them.

The current Eyjafjallajökull event is a relatively minor affair compared with many historic and prehistoric volcanic eruptions. Plant samples and sediments recovered from glaciers in Iceland and Canada indicate that a series of four volcanic eruptions in the tropics during the late thirteenth century might have been responsible for triggering a global cooling event which led to the so-called *Little Ice Age* in Europe (although a prolonged period of decreased sun-spot activity has also been implicated). Ash, sulphuric acid and aerosols released into the atmosphere during the 1991 eruption of Mount Pinatubo in the Philippines reflected sunlight back into space, lowering global temperatures for a couple of years. The same happened following the infamous Krakatoa eruption of 1883. It has also been suggested that volcanic eruptions led to disastrous famines in Europe from 1315–17, and in Russia from 1601–03. Far more disastrously, 65 million years ago, at the end of the Cretaceous period, the recently formed volcanic Deccan Traps in India might have been partially responsible (along with the more famous asteroid or comet impact which occurred at around the same time) for the mass-extinction event that saw off most of the dinosaurs.

In the grand scheme of volcanoes, Eyjafjallajökull could be seen as something of a damp squib. But, in this case, the squib's very dampness goes some way to explaining the effect it has had on the air transportation system. The name *Eyja-fjalla-jökull* means *islands-mountain-glacier* in Icelandic. The name says it all: the volcano in question is buried under an ice cap. When the volcano erupted, melt-water from the glacier fell into the crater and vaporised, adding significantly to the explosive effect. To make matters worse, Iceland's position directly beneath the Jet Stream means that ash emitted by the volcano has spread farther and quicker than it otherwise would have. Eyjafjallajökull might have been a damp squib, but she packed plenty of bang per buck.

It's astonishing how ash and other solid particles can be carried such great distances through the atmosphere. I've witnessed the phenomenon first-hand on two occasions. The first time was as I was walking home from school through Birkenhead town centre in the 1980s. The sun hadn't yet set, but, as I reached the roundabout at Charing Cross, the whole town, and the sky itself, suddenly turned an eerie yellow, as if illuminated by some massive sodium streetlight. It was totally disconcerting; one of the strangest experiences of my life. The next morning, local news reports explained how sands from the Sahara Desert had fallen on to the centre of Manchester, forty miles to the east. The second time was in March 2006. Jen and I were on holiday in Sicily. After breakfast one morning, I went out on to our hotel room balcony to read a book, but found the table and chairs covered in grit. I naturally assumed it was volcanic ash from nearby Etna, but the exasperated cleaning lady who arrived moments later soon put me straight: "Sahara!" she said, taking up her broom, shaking her head, and muttering away under her breath in Italian.

I'm not the only person to have walked on Saharan sands without having visited mainland Africa. In 1846, Charles Darwin wrote a short paper for the *Journal of the Geological Society of London* entitled *An account of the Fine Dust which often falls on Vessels in the Atlantic Ocean*. In it, he writes:

On the 16th of January (1833) [it was actually 1832], *when the Beagle was ten miles off the N.W. end of St. Jago* [modern-day Santiago, Cape Verde Islands], *some very fine dust was found adhering to the under side of the horizontal wind-vane at the mast-head; it appeared to have been filtered by the gauze from the air, as the ship lay inclined to the wind. The wind had been for twenty-four hours previously E.N.E., and hence, from the position of the ship, the dust probably came from the coast of Africa. The atmosphere was so hazy that the visible horizon was only one mile distant. During our stay of three weeks at St. Jago (to February 8th) the wind was N.E., as is always the case during this time of the year; the atmosphere was often hazy, and very fine dust was almost constantly falling, so that the astronomical instruments were roughened and a little injured. The dust collected on the Beagle was excessively fine-grained, and of a reddish brown colour; it does not effervesce with acids; it easily fuses under the blowpipe into a black or gray bead.*

Darwin goes on to describe how the dust he gathered contained considerable quantities of minute aquatic organisms known as *Infusoria*. He concludes that, while the types of *Infusoria* found didn't suggest an African origin for the dust, the wind direction at the time, which he associated with the seasonal *Harmattan* wind blowing from the Sahara, clearly did. He confesses that his findings present an enigma, but concludes:

the circumstance of such quantities of dust being periodically blown, year after year, over so immense an area in the Atlantic Ocean, is interesting, as showing by how apparently inefficient a cause a widely extended deposit may be in process of formation;

This is so typical of Darwin: inefficient, apparently random causes resulting in order. He's talking about geology, but he could easily be talking about evolution— even though he won't publish *On the Origin of Species* for another thirteen years. Interesting though the dispersal of such dust was to Darwin the geologist, far more interesting, I suspect, was the dispersal of *Infusoria* to Darwin the evolutionary biologist. Darwin had an abiding interest in any mechanisms by which organisms might be dispersed over great distances. But he would have been astonished to learn just how far the wind-borne African dusts he observed can spread.

In 2006, a paper in the journal *Environmental Research Letters* explained how dust from Africa regularly crosses the Atlantic Ocean and falls on South America. Entitled *The Bodélé depression: a single spot in the Sahara that provides most of the mineral dust to the Amazon forest*, the paper describes how around 40 million tons of dust are transported each year from the Sahara to the Amazon basin. The paper suggests that this dust is an important source of minerals for the Amazon rain forest, going so far as to suggest that the health and productivity of the rain forest is *dependent on* the transport of these minerals from the Sahara.

We live on a fascinating, complex planet.

Up at the trig point, save for a few pale clouds to the east, the sky is unblemished. There's so much sky up here. People talk of *landscapes* and *seascapes*, but many of the best are just as much *sky-scapes*. Like up here, where sky is half of everything I can see.

It's so clear up here this afternoon. It seems perverse, when all the talk in the news is of ash in the atmosphere. But most of the ash has spread so widely as to be invisible. Nevertheless, weather forecasters are predicting spectacular sunsets with characteristic purple fringes—*volcanic lavender*—caused when the red sunset blends with blue light scattered by the ash. Smoke from heather-burning can have a similar effect.

Provided there aren't too many of them, tiny particles suspended in fluids—that is, in liquids and gases—tend to scatter blue light. You see this phenomenon all the time, without even realising it: cigar smoke, moped exhausts, Houseman's *blue remembered hills*. Australia's Blue Mountains, which another Shropshire lad, Charles Darwin, visited in 1836, really do appear to have a blue tinge to them. Jen and I also visited the Blue Mountains years ago: the haze is very noticeable. It's caused by the scattering of sunlight by airborne chemicals emitted by the local eucalyptus trees. Even the blue colour of my eyes is caused by light-scattering particles suspended in a transparent layer in my irises; people with dark eyes have too many of these particles for the scattering to occur.

It was Charles Darwin's friend, the unfortunate John Tyndall, who first looked in detail at the scattering of light in *turbid*—that is, *cloudy*—fluids. Indeed, the phenomenon is now known as the *Tyndall effect*, or *Tyndall scattering*, in his honour. He was by no means the first scientist to consider such scattering, but he was the first to perform meticulous experiments to investigate it, using apparatus similar to that which he used to measure the heat-absorption properties of different atmospheric gases. He documented his findings in a paper submitted to the Royal Society in 1868. The title of Tyndall's paper reveals another commonly observed phenomenon explained by the scattering of light: *On the Blue Colour of the Sky, the Polarization of Skylight, and on the Polarization of*

Light by Cloudy matter Generally.

Although, in his introduction, Tyndall says that he will reserve the historic treatment of the subject for a more fitting occasion, his paper gives due credit to a number of other scientists who considered the phenomenon before him. Tyndall explains:

> *The idea that the colour of the sky is due to the action of finely divided matter, rendering the atmosphere a turbid medium, through which we look at the darkness of space, dates as far back as Leonardo da Vinci. Newton conceived the colour to be due to exceedingly small water particles acting as thin plates. Goethe's experiments in connexion with this subject are well known and exceedingly instructive.*

Having investigated the scattering of light by various gases, Tyndall hypothesises:

> *That water-particles, if they could be obtained in this exceedingly fine state of division, would produce the same* [scattering and polarizing] *effects, does not admit of reasonable doubt. And that they must exist in this condition in the higher regions of the atmosphere is, I think, certain. At all events, no other assumption than this is necessary to completely account for the firmamental blue and the polarization of the sky.*

The physicist Lord Rayleigh later showed that, for particles considerably smaller than the wavelength of light, the amount of scattering is inversely proportional to the fourth power of the light's wavelength. Such scattering is now known as *Rayleigh scattering*, with the term *Tyndall scattering* being applied to scattering by larger particles. Rayleigh's inverse-power rule explains why scattered sunlight—and, therefore, the sky—appears blue, as opposed to red or green. Blue light has a shorter wavelength, so, according to Rayleigh's formula, the scattering of light from the blue end of the spectrum is far greater than that from the red end. This means that, if you look at the sky away from the direction of the sun, you will see a far greater proportion of blue scattered light—which is why the sky appears blue. Conversely, if you look towards the sun—especially when it's low in the sky, when its light is passing through more of the earth's atmosphere, so even more of the light from the blue end of the spectrum is being scattered in other directions—you will see a higher proportion of light from the red end of the spectrum. This explains why sunrises and sunsets are red.

A German-born physicist named Albert Einstein subsequently showed that light can be scattered by particles as small as the individual oxygen or nitrogen molecules that comprise the vast majority of the earth's atmosphere. It isn't strictly necessary, it turns out, to have a turbid medium for light-scattering to occur, although it certainly enhances the effect.

I turn north and head along the track. Now that I've noticed their absence, it seems strange not to have jet-tracks marring the sky. And that might not be their only effect on the environment. The extent to which aircraft vapour trails affect local surface temperatures has been the subject of debate for years. They can affect temperatures in two different and opposite ways. The additional cloud-cover created by the trails reflects some sunlight back into space, thereby decreasing local surface temperatures—although, clearly, this can only happen during daylight hours. Conversely, the additional cloud-cover will add temporarily to the local *greenhouse effect*, retaining more of the heat radiated back towards space from the planet surface. This second effect would work throughout the day. The presence of vapour trails should, therefore, lead to increased local temperatures at night, and less increased (or quite possibly decreased) local temperatures during the day. In other words, vapour trails should lead to smaller local diurnal temperature ranges. But how to test such a prediction?

An opportunity for such a test arose as a result of the three-day grounding of all commercial aircraft in the United States following the 9/11 terrorist attacks in 2001. The grounding allowed scientists, after the event, to compare diurnal temperature differences across the United States over the three days with historical records going back 30 years. They found that, while the aircraft were grounded, and there were no vapour trails in the sky, the diurnal temperature range increased by an average of 1.1°C. Furthermore, the increase tended to be higher in areas which usually had higher concentrations of vapour trails. In other words, it looks as if vapour trails might indeed have a measurable effect on local diurnal temperature ranges.

That's quite enough blue-sky thinking for the time being. Spring is here! I think I might head down towards the fields at the edge of the Moor to see if the wheatears have returned.

Crash

According to the old joke, we don't have climate in Britain; we have weather. Boy, do we have weather! April has been a real stinker: *the shittiest on record*, according to the Met Office. I paraphrase. It's been abysmal: snow, rain, more rain, wind, cold. March might have been the third warmest on record, but April has been the coldest for 23 years, and the wettest *since records began*—over a century ago. Perversely, the average April temperature was colder than that of March. Britain, let me remind you, is in the northern hemisphere: it's supposed to be getting warmer at this time of year.

The rain was relentless yesterday, as was the wind. I had to brave the elements to retrieve our wheelie-bin, which was making an unscheduled tour of the driveway. The gutter on our outhouse blew off, and the window at the bottom of the stairs—one of the few old windows we thought could still be relied on—started letting in water faster than the *Titanic*. Such are the delights of owning an old house 750 feet up in the Pennines. Meanwhile, to add insult to injury, there's been an unprecedented spring heat-wave on the continent. A tornado hit Toulouse yesterday. It serves them right.

Everyone's been cursing the weather forecasters. I know it's unfair, but it goes with the territory. I have to say, though, they called it right yesterday: they predicted a change in the weather, and here it is! Today, the last day of the wettest of all Aprils, dawned clear and bright, albeit with a stiff, south-easterly breeze. About bloody time! There was nothing for it: I dug out my wellington boots, and headed up on to the Moor.

I'm in search of swallows and wheatears this morning. I saw my first swallow of the so-called summer back on 12th April. It was flying through a hail-storm over our house, no doubt wondering what the hell was going on. Welcome back to Blighty! But swallows, no matter how many, don't make a summer until I've seen them flying above the Moor. As for the wheatears, I know they've been sighted down south, so I must be in with a chance.

I climb up the sunken track on Little Moor, and over the stile on to the Moor proper. Wellies were definitely a good call. Improvised streams trickle down the hill. *Rivulets*: a favourite word. Within seconds, a swallow flops over the wall and twists away across the heather. That makes it official: winter is most definitely over, whatever the weather. I pass below the ruined building at *Johnny House*, and head towards the second stile. Yes, this is more like it: warm sunshine and a brisk breeze; a promise of a summer to come.

I think of poor Admiral FitzRoy. He certainly took more than his fair share of stick for his weather forecasts. In many ways, he was years ahead of his time. In his younger days, as plain Captain FitzRoy, he had taken Charles Darwin around the world aboard *HMS Beagle*. He had first taken command of the ship on her previous voyage, following the suicide of the *Beagle*'s then captain, Pringle Stokes. Stokes, it seemed, had been unable to bear the loneliness of command in the desolate waters of Tierra del Fuego. He botched his suicide attempt with a poorly aimed pistol shot to the head, taking ten days to die. FitzRoy was painfully conscious of the fact that his uncle, Viscount Castlereagh, had also committed suicide. He was worried that he might have inherited a familial suicidal trait, and that, like Stokes, he might find the loneliness of command in the South Atlantic too much to bear. Unable to fraternise too closely with *Beagle*'s officers and crew, FitzRoy sought permission from the Admiralty to take a gentleman companion with him on the ship's second voyage. It was thanks to two suicides, therefore, that Charles Darwin ended up travelling the world, and becoming the most important scientist in the history of biology.

Robert FitzRoy was a perfectionist. He was also no mean amateur scientist, and an enthusiastic early-adopter of new technologies. *HMS Beagle* was one of the *Cherokee* class of ships, unaffectionately known as *coffin brigs*, on account of their unfortunate tendency to sink. Before her second voyage, however, FitzRoy had a number of modifications made to the ship to improve her seaworthiness. These included raising the upper deck, installing a new design of rudder and a third mast, having her bottom coppered to prevent barnacles from boring into the wood, and installing the first proper lightning-conductor on a Royal Navy ship. As we have already seen, to ensure accuracy of longitudinal measurements on what was primarily a surveying voyage, FitzRoy took no less than twenty-two expensive ship's chronometers with him on the trip. The charts he brought back from the voyage were phenomenally accurate, and could still quite safely be used today.

After the second *Beagle* voyage, FitzRoy was briefly the Tory Member of Parliament for Durham, and the Acting Conservator of the River Mersey. In 1843, however, he was appointed the second Governor of New Zealand. This was a thankless role, in which he had to try to balance the needs and demands of the white settlers with those of the indigenous Maoris, with little or no support from his superiors back home. Honourable almost to a fault, FitzRoy's sense of justice made him a figure of hatred with the settlers. They were particularly incensed when he forgave a Maori chieftain who had massacred nineteen white prisoners during a land dispute. FitzRoy's justification for siding with the Maoris was that it had been the deceased settlers who had started the trouble. Outraged, their fellow settlers burnt FitzRoy's effigy in the streets. Having exceeded his authority in a number of areas—an unfortunate habit he had also been reprimanded for on the *Beagle* voyage— FitzRoy was recalled to Britain.

After a few more naval postings, and promotion to Vice Admiral, FitzRoy was, in 1854, put in charge of the nascent Meteorological Office. The purpose of the office was to provide statistical weather data. As always, however, FitzRoy was soon exceeding his brief. He was convinced that many sailors' lives could be saved, were it possible to *predict* the weather. So he began distributing barometers to ships' captains and ports.

Then, on the 25th and 26th October 1859—a month before FitzRoy's former shipmate finally published *On the Origin of Species*—a mighty storm passed along the west coast of Britain. It moved up from the English Channel, around Wales, across Liverpool Bay, and on up to Scotland. It is thought to have been the most severe storm to hit Britain in the entire nineteenth century, reaching force 12, *hurricane force*, on the scale invented by FitzRoy's former boss Sir Francis Beaufort. The great storm of 1859 was responsible for the loss of around 800 lives, and the wrecking of 133 ships. Over half the lives lost—around 459—resulted from the loss of a single ship, *The Royal Charter*, a 2,700-tonne steam clipper en route to Liverpool from Melbourne. Having tried and failed to take on board a Liverpool pilot, the ship's captain, Thomas Taylor, decided to attempt to weather the storm by dropping anchor off the east coast of Anglesey—a coast very dear to my heart. But, early in the morning of 26th October, first one and then the other of the ship's anchor chains snapped. *The Royal Charter* was driven on to rocks just north of the fishing village of Moelfre, and broke apart. Only 39 passengers and crew managed to struggle ashore. The rest either drowned or were dashed against the rocks.

The wreck of *The Royal Charter* was a national sensation. Charles Dickens visited Moelfre shortly afterwards to report on the aftermath for his magazine. His piece was later reproduced in his collection *The Uncommercial Traveller*. The incident provided FitzRoy with the strongest argument he needed for *forecasting the weather* (a term which he himself coined). Fifteen land stations were quickly established, which used the new electrical telegraph system to send FitzRoy daily weather reports. Just a year after the dreadful wreck, FitzRoy's daily weather forecasts began to be published in the *Times* newspaper.

Modern-day meteorologists aided by supercomputers capable of crunching billions of data items per second still struggle to give accurate weather forecasts. FitzRoy, with his fifteen daily readings, never stood a chance. His Met Office weather forecasts became a national running joke. In many ways, with considerable less justification, modern weather forecasts still are.

FitzRoy's perfectionism, his highly strung temperament, and, very likely, the public criticism of his weather forecasts goaded him to work harder and harder. In April 1865, he seems to have had a nervous breakdown. On 30th April—147 years ago this very day—he locked himself in his dressing room, took up his razor, and slit his throat. Tragically, FitzRoy's fear of a hereditary suicidal trait seems to have had some foundation.

Poor Robert FitzRoy: a great captain eclipsed by his shipmate; a complex, tragic figure, who deserves to be ranked alongside our greatest seamen; a man nowadays remembered more for his failings than his many achievements. Unlike Darwin and the *Beagle*, it seems unlikely that FitzRoy will ever make it on to the back of a banknote. But he does at least have one fitting modern memorial, one which I'm sure would have pleased him. In 2002, in an international accord to agree standards between the Atlantic-coast countries of Britain, France, Spain, Portugal and Morocco, the shipping area formerly known as *Finisterre* was renamed *FitzRoy* in honour of the world's first professional weatherman.

I reach the second stile and climb over. The wall to my left becomes more tumbledown, giving way to fence. Something catches my eye in the field beyond. A white blob flits up from the ground, disappearing behind a clump of rushes. Seconds later, another white flash, then a third. There's no mistaking those white flashes: *wheatears!* They're back!

The birds skip and flit teasingly ahead of me, as ever keeping just too far away to allow me to take a decent photo. Two males and a female. The males are definitely not hitting it off. One of them chases his rival away, returns to perch briefly on a fence-post, then flits ahead on to the wall. He's wearing his finest breeding plumage: grey crown, nape and mantle, pink chest, black stripes along his wings, white stripes across his brows, black bandit-mask across his eyes. Just like in my *I-SPY* book! Neat, clipped and compact: as dapper as ever. It's hard to believe this bird has just flown all the way from sub-Saharan Africa.

I continue along the track, the remaining pair of wheatears leading the way. When I reach the stile to the fields above Dike Lane, I turn uphill to explore a narrow gully which I identified from online photographs recently. My eyes scour the ground. I'm looking for signs of an event which took place on this very spot 75 years ago, if the deductions of amateur researchers published on the internet are correct:

On the morning of 12th December 1936, a formation of seven Handley Page Heyford Mk III heavy night bombers from 102 Squadron left RAF Aldergrove in County Antrim. They were en route to their home base at the newly opened RAF Finningley near Doncaster (the future site of Robin Hood Airport). The bombers and their crews had spent the last few weeks in Northern Ireland, training over Lough Neagh. They had been scheduled to return to England the previous day, but had been prevented from flying due to adverse weather conditions. Their flight plan took them east, across the Irish Sea to Morecambe Bay, before changing course south east towards Finningley.

Less than a decade before the Royal Air Force developed the capability to carpet-bomb German cities almost off the face of the planet, their state-of-the-art bombers were biplanes with open cockpits and gun turrets. It took a second dreadful world war to provide the impetus needed to innovate. The Heyford bomber turned out to be the last of its breed, being declared obsolete in July 1939, just two months before the outbreak of war.

To modern eyes, the Heyford was an ungainly affair. Unusually for a biplane, its fuselage was attached to the upper pair of wings, giving the aircraft a decidedly *top-heavy* appearance. But there was method in this apparent madness, as the design afforded the nose- and rear-gunners a wider field-of-view, providing the bombers with better protection against fighter aircraft.

The formation of Heyfords crossed the Irish Sea at 4,000 feet without incident, but then encountered a dense, freezing sea-fog over Morecambe Bay. The aircraft adjusted their courses towards Finningley as planned, but visibility became even worse. The pilots lost sight of each other's aircraft, and the formation was broken. The pilot of aircraft serial number K6900, Sgt V.C. Otter, asked his wireless operator to try to get a bearing on the Finningley ground station. They were out of luck: the ground station's transmitter was down for routine annual maintenance. A momentary break in the fog then revealed that the aircraft's wings were coated in a thick layer of ice. Otter increased altitude as a precaution and continued in the general direction of Finningley.

How cold must it have been, sitting in an open cockpit, in freezing fog, with only a low windscreen, flight-suit, leather helmet, woolly scarf, and goggles for protection? The journey must have seemed interminable.

Then, at around 12:45, Otter's co-pilot, Sgt D.G. Church, suddenly yelled, "Get up!" A dark mass appeared out of the fog. Otter attempted an emergency climb, but the ice on the aircraft's wings prevented it. K6900 ploughed into the hill, skidded 100 yards up the slope, breaking apart as it ran, and burst into flames.

Otter came to with his scarf and fur-lined goggles on fire. He fell out of what was left of the cockpit and rolled in the snow to put himself out. Having called and searched in vain for the other three crew, his wrist and ankle badly injured, Otter hobbled his way downhill as far as he could before taking shelter behind a farm shed. Some time later, he heard calls in the fog, and shouted for help. Locals had witnessed the crash and were coming to the rescue. They informed Otter that he had crashed near Hebden Bridge in Yorkshire. Some of the rescue party headed up towards the crash site to look for the missing crew, while others helped Otter down the hill to the local post office. Otter's facial injuries were so bad that the postmistress who dressed his wounds turned her mirrors to face the walls so he couldn't see himself in them.

Two of Otter's crewmates, C.V. Bodenham and P.G. Clements, were killed in the crash. The third, his co-pilot, D.G. Church, died in the ambulance as he and Otter were being taken to Halifax Royal Infirmary. Otter was subsequently moved between a series of RAF hospitals, where he underwent an extensive course of plastic surgery for the burns to his face and hands. He returned to his squadron two years later, but was pronounced unfit for flying duties. He did, however, remain in the RAF until 1969, reaching the rank of Air Vice Marshal.

Of the seven Heyford aircraft that took off from Aldergrove that day, only one made it directly to Finningley. Of the others, two made successful forced landings in fields, two crashed during similar attempted landings (their crews survived), and one crashed near Oldham, the crew having bailed out.

I remember my late friend Mary once mentioning a bomber crash on the Moor, "up near Johnny House", when she was a girl. Could this be the place? The researchers who posted the photographs on the internet certainly think so, and they seem to have done their homework. They even brought metal-detectors, and unearthed lumps of metal and glass, including several lumps of molten aluminium. Good for them! Entropy hasn't won just yet: the signs are still there, if you're prepared to look hard enough. But I don't have a metal-detector. All I can see is a long furrow—a drainage ditch, most likely—and a rocky mound covered in moor-grass.

I turn to take in the view over towards Old Town and Heptonstall. It's hard to imagine biplanes flying in these skies, not so very long ago. It's harder still to think that three young men were mortally injured in a horrific crash on or near this very spot.

FitzRoy was right: accurate weather forecasts can save lives. The lives of airmen, as well as sailors.

Boundary

The last week in September. Clear blue sky, hazy near the sun. Orion was hanging high over our gate an hour before sunrise this morning. The first sighting of Orion marks the official start of autumn, as far as I'm concerned. But it feels far from autumnal today—so much so that I'm on the Moor in my shirt-sleeves.

I take the stone-flagged path through the bog. For a change, I don't turn uphill towards the trig point. Today, I've decided to pay my respects to a venerable old maid. I carry on along the track beside the drystone wall at the edge of the Moor. I can only just see over the wall into the field beyond. Rooks are dibbing for invertebrates. You can always depend on there being rooks. I pause at the gate to admire the view of the semi-ruined stone barn with the two mature sycamores behind, the only sizeable trees visible on this side of the valley. To their right, across the valley, Stoodley Pike and its eponymous monument provide the official backdrop to the Upper Calder Valley.

I continue along the track. My destination rises slowly

into view: a thin, square-based standing-stone, almost seven feet tall, tapering slightly towards the top, leaning slightly towards the west. *Churn Milk Joan.*

If local folklore is to believed, Churn Milk Joan was a milk-maid who was caught in a blizzard on the Moor, and froze to death on this very spot. The stone is her monument. She was fetching milk to Mytholmroyd, or possibly Mount Skip, from some isolated, plague-ridden village across the Moor. Or perhaps not. Some say she died here and was eaten by foxes. Or she actually turned into this very stone—tall lass, our Joan. Or she was a witch, whose name wasn't Joan, but Peg. One thing's for sure: Ted Hughes wrote a poem about her. Ted Hughes wrote poems about most things around here. He seems to have been as confused as the rest of us about who Churn Milk Joan might actually have been.

I'm going to go out on a limb and say that Churn Milk Joan never actually existed. Furthermore, I'm fairly confident her standing-stone doesn't spin round three times on New Year's Eve, as the bells of St Michael's church in Mytholmroyd ring in the valley below. But I'm just an incorrigible sceptic, so don't mind me.

I reach the stone and walk slowly around it, shading my eyes from the sun. Despite my scepticism, there's something undeniably magical about standing-stones, irrespective of the dodgy supernatural stories inevitably attached to them. Any large, carved stone demands attention: drinking troughs, milestones, even old gateposts. But Churn Milk Joan demands more attention than most, standing, as she does, at a meeting of tracks in the middle of nowhere; a rare vertical in this horizontal landscape. You couldn't possibly walk by without paying your respects: it would feel rude.

Joan's four sides are rough and uneven. She might almost have been formed naturally, but her approximate symmetry and large length-to-width ratio make it seem more likely she was shaped by long-forgotten hands for some long-forgotten purpose. Certainly, human hands, both ancient and modern, have left their marks on her surface. Two feet or so above the ground, on Joan's eastern face, surveyors have carved a three-legged benchmark symbol to act as a reference point. Immediately below and above this mark, Joan bears two far more ancient scars: a pair of inverted cup-shaped holes. She has five such holes in total, four on this face, one on the south: pre-historic rock-art, carved in the Bronze Age or late Neolithic. Churn Milk Joan, it turns out, is an extremely old maid indeed.

I run my fingers around one of the cup-marks, a hollow in the rock a couple of inches across. It thrills me to think that the first person to place their fingers, Doubting-Thomas-like, into Joan's side lived here, on the Moor—if, indeed, it was a moor back then—2,500–4,800 years ago. The marks themselves are a mystery, their purpose lost in the entropy. But such marks are not uncommon, there being several hundred examples in Britain alone, including others elsewhere on the Moor. They seem to be associated with ancient burial sites, and are often surrounded by shallow 'rings' pecked into the rock. I've searched in vain for any such rings on Churn

Milk Joan. There are a few faint marks, but to describe them as rings would be wishful thinking in the extreme. Perhaps they were never there, or perhaps they too have been lost to the entropy.

Try this for scale: the people who carved the cup-marks on Churn Milk Joan would have been more ancient to Julius Caesar than Julius Caesar is to us. Forget spinning stones and milk-maids eaten by foxes, aren't physical, unexplained and, most likely, forever inexplicable marks, twice as old as recorded history, far more satisfactory mysteries to enthral our minds? Why waste your sense of wonder on stuff that isn't true, when there are genuine wonders aplenty in this world?

I stand back to take the obligatory photos. Joan is looking particularly photogenic this afternoon, casting a long, autumnal shadow to the north east: the Moor's very own sundial. But her upright position is relatively new. She was moved here to mark the boundary between the townships of Wadsworth and Midgley some time before the start of the seventeenth century. To her west, where I usually walk, the Moor is officially known as Wadsworth Moor; to the east, it's Midgley Moor. To me, the sheep, and the grouse, however, such invisible, man-made boundaries are meaningless: the two conjoined 'moors' are simply *the Moor*. But boundaries were important to the commoners who held certain rights on the moors, and to the Lords Savile and Lacy who claimed ownership and enclosed parts of them. Encroachments occurred on either side. Legal disputes arose concerning commons grazing, water, and turbary (peat-gathering) rights. In the end, maps were commissioned to agree and define boundaries, some of them being drawn up by none other than Christopher Saxton, England's most famous early cartographer. On the ground itself, stones and cairns were set up to mark the agreed boundaries, with some pre-existing markers being roped in for good measure. The markers had, or were given, names such as Blether Hill, the Greenwood Stone, Resby Mere, Farror's Boulder, Lad Law, and Wadsworth Law. Churn Milk Joan was given the name Savile's Law—a *law* being a small hill, burial mound, or, as in this case, pile of stones. A few large stones still lie half-buried in the peat at Joan's feet.

I put my camera away, and perform the traditional ritual, standing on the stone nearest to Joan, and reaching up to grope in the small hollow on top of her head. I find a couple of coins left by previous pilgrims, two pennies, and replace them with coins of slightly higher value from my own pocket, two two-pence pieces. Some say that Churn Milk Joan is an ancient penny stone, where, in times of plague, people would leave coins soaked in vinegar in exchange for wares to be dropped off at the stone. I, of course, am not so sure, but I'm all for maintaining harmless tradition.

Out of pocket to the tune of two pence, I bid Joan farewell, and head north, uphill, along the track through the heather. I'm following the agreed parish boundary now, left foot in Wadsworth, right in Midgley. Saxton's old maps refer to the once-disputed lands either side of the boundary as *commons*, not *moors*. The distinction speaks volumes. They got away with it, those landowners, enclosing the commons, depriving the commoners of their ancient rights. Modern-day, right-leaning politicians keep banging on about repealing human rights acts and European treaties; you never hear them demanding the repeal of the glaringly corrupt Enclosures Acts.

Enclosure of common land goes all the way back to medieval times, but it took off in earnest in the mid-eighteenth century with the passing of thousands of *Inclosure Acts*. In a 2001 paper, *Common Rights in Land in England, 1475–1839*, Gregory Clark and Anthony Clark used statistical analyses to estimate the amount of common land lost to enclosure. They concluded that, during the years 1750 to 1840, the amount of common land in England decreased from around 20% of all land to around 5%. That's the loss of an area roughly the same size as all three Ridings of Yorkshire plus Lincolnshire combined. Talk about common theft!

After a few hundred metres, I veer off the track to the right in search of a second ancient monument. Despite its large size, it proves surprisingly difficult to locate. I wander back and forth through the heather, and am about to give up, when I spot a low, heathery mound topped with a few loose stones. It looks for all the world like an oversized grouse-shooters' butt. It is, in fact, a Bronze Age burial cairn of indeterminate age—most likely somewhere between 3,000 and 4,000 years old. The Ordnance Survey map labels it *Miller's Grave*.

Once again, local folklore has tales to tell. It always does. The Miller in question, so it's said, was a miller by trade, not by name. His name was, in fact—or, more likely, *in fable*—Lee. He committed suicide, and, as a result, was buried in unconsecrated ground near some crossroads in Midgley. But the locals were freaked out, having to pass near the grave every day. So, one night, they formed a mob to disinter the body, which they carried on to the Moor and reburied in the prehistoric cairn that now bears the miller's job title. Far from improving the situation, the removal of the miller's body only made matters worse. The villagers now became convinced that his unquiet ghost roamed the Moor. So they dug up his body once again and reburied it Heptonstall churchyard. I can't help thinking the good people of Midgley could have avoided a whole lot of fuss, had they simply seen fit to give the poor miller a decent, Christian burial in the first place.

Alternatively, there are those who would have you believe that Miller's Grave was named after Much the Miller's son, one of Robin Hood's *Merry Men*. This, presumably, is on account of the large boulder one-hundred metres to the west, *Robin Hood's Penny Stone*. We have a lot of penny stones around here.

I climb the tumulus and look down into it. A large, cleft glacial boulder sits in the middle of the mound, surrounded by loosely piled stones. Local amateur antiquarians have observed that the cleft aligns with Nab Hill, a low summit on the skyline a few miles to the north. But I can't help noticing that, looking the other way, it also aligns with Blackstone Edge to the south. Most clefts will align with something or other, if you extend the line far enough.

What an isolated, lonely place! I can think of worse

places to be buried. Hey, there's an idea: my paternal grandmother's family name was Miller! But no, Jen and I have already booked our final resting place in the graveyard at Wainsgate Chapel, on the very edge of the Moor. Other than the pile of stones, there isn't much to see here, but the burial mound is hauntingly atmospheric—or it would be, were it not for the eyesore of the local wind power-station flailing away to the north east. I admire the unobtrusiveness of tumuli, the way they blend into the landscape, slowly becoming part of it. Entropy in action. Then I smirk, recalling a coffee-break tale from my archaeological dig in Shetland back in 1985, about the archaeologist who spent an entire summer excavating a 'barrow', only to discover that it was a drumlin: a natural, glacier-eroded hillock. Needless to say, he didn't find any Bronze Age artefacts.

I turn and walk the short distance to Robin Hood's Penny Stone. This is no archaeological site, but a natural geological feature. I have to say, though, I'm confused. I'm guessing this massive, rounded boulder is an erratic, dumped in the middle of what was to become the Moor as glaciers retreated. But this area is supposed to have remained glacier-free during the most recent Ice Age. That's why the valleys around here are so steep: they were carved by melt-water, not glaciers. So presumably this rock must have been deposited here during an earlier glacial period. Or perhaps not. Perhaps it's not an erratic after all. I'm pretty hopeless when it comes to geology.

I stand on one of the smaller rocks at its base to

inspect the top of the boulder. A shallow, rain-filled basin about one foot in diameter contains a number of copper coins. I remove a two-pence piece and replace it with a ten. 'Penny' stones, my arse! There's inflation for you!

No prizes for guessing that local folklore has an explanation for why Robin Hood's Penny Stone is so named. I'll spare you the details. I'm going to go out on a limb once more, and say that Robin Hood never actually existed either—although, if he had, he would surely have had something to say about the theft of common land.

I cut back across the heather, towards the track. It proves surprisingly difficult to find. Either the track's course has altered since I left it, or I've got the direction wrong. Perhaps both. When you're standing in heather, one clump looks pretty much like the next, and paths through it can be invisible from only a few metres away. I'm debating whether I should head more to the left, when I step on to the track without even seeing it coming. This *is* the same track, isn't it? I think so. It seems to be heading in roughly the right direction, so I turn along it. It's very easy to become disorientated on open, featureless moor.

I pass a couple of small, upright stones at the side of the track. Boundary-markers, perhaps, or maybe just stones. And then a second large standing-stone rises into view: the *Greenwood Stone*. Not as tall as Churn Milk Joan, only about four feet, but still an eye-catchingly vertical marker. Greenwood: a good, honest, Calder Valley surname, like Crabtree, Butterworth, and Pickles. Hobbit surnames. As with Churn Milk Joan, human hands have made their marks on the surface of the Greenwood Stone. But these marks were made practically yesterday, simply recording the year in which they were carved: 1775. The year in which certain colonials began kicking up a fuss over the Pond.

I glance south, and am surprised to see Robin Hood's Penny Stone and Miller's Grave clearly in view a few hundred metres away. I must have taken a very roundabout route to get from there to here. Having failed to learn my lesson, I leave the track and cut across the heather once more. The view opens up, there's a bit of a clamber down a bank, and I find myself standing on another track. It takes me a couple of seconds to realise where I am: back in familiar territory, on the track along the edge from the trig point. I look north, across Dimmin Dale, up to the trig point on top of High Brown Knoll. A short distance to its right, I can just make out a third standing-stone—another parish boundary-marker— silhouetted against the skyline. I briefly consider making my way up to it, but then remember that Wadsworth Parish is the second largest in the country, and its boundary is over twenty miles in circumference.

You have to draw a line somewhere.

Grandeur

Early morning, mid-May. Through the new stile, along the paved track through the bog, and up the rise. Sheep and lambs scatter in pairs. Rooks rise and wheel. A rabbit flees. The chill, north-easterly breeze is stronger up here. Perhaps I should have worn my fleece after all.

Pipits and skylarks take flight at the top of the rise. I skirt the edge of the quarry and follow the track through the heather towards the trig point. A curlew pipes distantly on the wind. Up ahead, hidden grouse admonish me to *go-back!* Fat chance! Not on a day like today.

I reach the trig point, and touch it to make it official. *Bracing!* For some reason, my usually reliable coat is refusing to turn the wind today. I should definitely have worn my fleece. But who cares? I take out my flask and make myself a brew, using the top of the trig point as a table. I sup slowly, taking in the view. I can see for miles.

In case you haven't already guessed, I love it up here.

A few weeks ago, I revisited Durham, my old university

town, for the first time in a quarter of a century. It was the strangest experience. I walked the once-familiar streets as if in a dream. No, not in a dream; it was as if I were wandering around somewhere I'd dreamt about many times, and was finally visiting in the waking world. "This place is actually real!" I kept saying to Jen. I couldn't get over the fact that everything was in colour, that there was warmth, that there were noises and smells, and, most surprisingly of all, that I could have forgotten so much. Everywhere I looked, there was something uncannily familiar, yet bright, and new, and real.

I feel the same way every time I come up on to the Moor. There is wind, there is mud, the sky is huge and wide and bright—even when it's grey. There are sounds and smells. There is heat and cold. This place is *real*. This is how it feels to be on the Moor. To be alive. How could I have forgotten? It's only been a few days.

Spiritual, some people call feelings like these. I try to avoid the word. Its religious connotations make me wary, even though its Latin root, *spirare*, simply means 'to breathe'. *Inspirational* has the same root. How did such a physical act as filling your lungs with air molecules become associated with your immaterial, non-existent 'spirit'? In what way does invoking such a spirit make your most deeply personal experiences more meaningful? Come to think of it, how the hell does referring to a person's 'spirit' help to explain anything?

No, *spiritual* doesn't resonate with me. Not in that sense. It would, though, I think, have resonated with my fellow Pennine-wayfarer, the seventeenth-century religious dissenter George Fox.

Fox was convinced that God's message comes directly to individuals through personal insights, rather than through a religious intermediary. No preachers or priests for him. He founded the *Religious Society of Friends*, more commonly known as the *Quakers*, who believe in sudden divine inspiration—there's that word again—or, in their parlance, *openings*. In 1652, in what Fox later described as the beginning of a new era, he experienced such an opening right here in the Pennines. It was a key moment in his life. He described the event in his autobiography:

> *As we travelled we came near a very great hill, called Pendle Hill, and I was moved of the Lord to go up to the top of it; which I did with difficulty, it was so very steep and high. When I was come to the top, I saw the sea bordering upon Lancashire. From the top of this hill the Lord let me see in what places he had a great people to be gathered. As I went down, I found a spring of water in the side of the hill, with which I refreshed myself, having eaten or drunk but little for several days before.*

I take another sip of tea.

Had George Fox, as I'm sure he must have, turned his back for a moment on Lancashire and the Irish Sea, and directed his gaze inland, south east, beyond the town of Nelson, across the hills towards Halifax, he might have had an even more spiritual experience: he might well have laid eyes on the Moor. I can just make out the summit of Pendle Hill from here, through the gap above Bateman's reservoir at Widdop. Pendle is usually little more than a shadow, but, in this easterly, early morning light, I can make out a few features on its flank. Then the wind brings water to my eyes, and I have to turn away.

True story: when my primary school teachers used to go on about my 'soul' in our early morning, state-sponsored, religious indoctrination sessions—or *assemblies*, as they were officially called—I used to think they were referring to a physical organ in my body. I must have seen a basic anatomical diagram in a children's encyclopaedia somewhere. I had a reasonable idea what my brain, heart and lungs were for. I was aware of kidneys, but knew I had two of those, so they couldn't possibly be my soul. Which left my liver. I became convinced that my soul was a large, wedge-shaped organ on top of my tummy. The diagram I'd seen must have shown the organs in different colours, as I also got it into my head that my soul was purple. To this day, when somebody refers to a human soul, I can't help but imagine a purple, liver-shaped organ. Which means I'll probably never go to heaven. In fact, I'd bet my house on it, if I could think of a way to collect my winnings. To be honest, I'm still not entirely sure what my liver is for. I should look it up some time. But I have a book to finish first.

I breathe deeply, filling my lungs—lime green, if memory serves—with cold, fresh air, straight from the Irish Sea by way of Pendle. Yes, this is it all right: *the real thing*. Reality is where it's at. Accept no alternatives. Isn't life short enough already without wasting it filling our heads—and the heads of others—with talk of spirits, the supernatural, the paranormal, false histories, conspiracy theories, wild hypotheses, alternative therapies, *non sequiturs*, wishful thinking, and other patent nonsense? We only get a few precious years on this wonderful planet before we succumb to the entropy. Wouldn't it be better to spend them trying to appreciate the world for what it is, rather than being taken in by falsehoods?

I don't get it. Isn't reality good enough? When did appreciating the world for what it really is become *unromantic*—or, as some would have it, *soulless*? How can it ever be preferable to believe or invent stuff that isn't true? Did Sir Thomas Browne somehow *belittle* the ostrich when he demonstrated that it couldn't digest iron? Do I somehow belittle the peregrine falcon when I point out that her apparent exquisite design is a kludgily evolved compromise? Or the woman running on a treadmill when I describe her as a glorified fish? (I did say *glorified*, for Pete's sake!) Isn't it better to know that the wheatear is named for its *white arse*, and not for a wheat-coloured stripe near its ear? Isn't it better to know that standing-stones don't really spin around on New Year's Eve? Isn't it better to realise and accept that entropy always wins in the end, no matter how hard we might fight it? Isn't the truth infinitely preferable to the fanciful? Yes, by all means think fancifully occasionally—that's where many of our best ideas come from—but realise when you're doing it, and realise that extraordinary hypotheses require extraordinary evidence before they can be accepted. After which, they cease to be extraordinary—although, it's to be hoped, they will still retain their wonder.

Darwin knew. He got it. A more modest and humble revolutionary you couldn't hope to meet. Yet he allowed himself a moment's pride in the opening eight words of the final sentence of *On the Origin of Species*:

There is grandeur in this view of life…

Darwin hadn't *belittled* Nature by explaining how life evolves; he had revealed its true grandeur. All Nature is related. We weren't created through divine *fiat*, according to some incomprehensible, archetypal master plan; we got here on our own, through hard graft. It was tough, it was messy, but we got here. We are awesome.

The clock is ticking. Entropy approaches. You have a wonderful set of glorified-fish sense organs. You have a glorious, glorified-fish brain. There's a whole world out there for it—for you—to appreciate while you still can. So go for a walk. Have a look around you. Find stuff out. Read a book—a book about pigeons, or Vikings, or whatever takes your fancy, provided it's based in reality. And make it a priority. Life's too short to do otherwise.

And if somebody tells you, for example, that the twelfth thoracic vertebra is the location of the solar plexus chakra, either ignore them as a nut-job, or do them a favour and ask them what the hell they're on about. If they tell you, ask them to explain their answer. If they feign to offer further explanation, ask them how they know. If you haven't begun to smell bullshit by this stage, there's probably no hope for you. In which case, good luck to you, and don't mind me: I shall, I hope, still be up here, on the Moor, blissfully filling my lungs with ice-cold reality.

I put away my flask, take one more look at the view, then turn north. Perhaps I'll see the curlew I heard earlier. Most likely I'll see some grouse. Perhaps I'll see something new entirely. You never know.

That's the whole point.

.

About the Author

Richard Carter lives just below the Moor in Hebden Bridge, West Yorkshire. You can follow his latest adventures in the following ways:

Website: richardcarter.com
Newsletter: richardcarter.com/newsletter/
Twitter: @friendsofdarwin
Facebook: facebook.com/richardcarter.updates

Acknowledgements

Thanks to Jen Mulcahy for everything.

Thanks for the encouragement and feedback to: Neil Ansell, Jeff Barrett, Michael Barton, Maureen Brian, Gilly Carter, Norman Carter, Thony Christie, Adrian Cooper, Mike Dagley, Carolyn Farthing, GrrlScientist, Bill Heafield, Julian Hoffman, Karen James, Peter McGrath, the Mulcahy Clan, Ben Myers, Jen Pickles, Stense, Dave Whiteland, John S Wilkins, and Jessica Woollard.

Credits

References

For an extensive list of source material consulted during the writing of this book, please visit:

richardcarter.com/on-the-moor/references/

Postscripts

For a list of postscripts, corrections, clarifications, afterthoughts, and related paraphernalia, please visit:

richardcarter.com/on-the-moor/postscripts/

Printed in Great Britain
by Amazon

62287199R00183